IN DEFENCE OF THE ENLIGHTENMENT

Tzvetan Todorov is a Honorary Director of Research at the CNRS in Paris. Critic, philosopher and historian, he is the author of numerous books, including *Facing the Extreme* and *Hope and Memory*, which has been translated into eleven languages. He has also been a recipient of the international *Principe de Asturias* prize.

In Defence of the Enlightenment

TZVETAN TODOROV

*Translated from the French
by Gila Walker*

Atlantic Books
LONDON

First published in France in 2006 by Éditions Robert Laffont.

First published in English in hardback in Great Britain in 2009
by Atlantic Books, an imprint of Grove Atlantic Ltd.

This paperback edition published in Great Britain in 2010
by Atlantic Books, an imprint of Atlantic Books Ltd.

1 3 5 7 9 10 8 6 4 2

A CIP catalogue record for this book is available
from the British Library.

ISBN 978 1 84354 814 0

Designed and typeset by Lindsay Nash

Printed in Great Britain

Atlantic Books
An imprint of Atlantic Books Ltd
Ormond House
26–27 Boswell Street
London WC1N 3JZ

www.atlantic-books.co.uk

Contents

IN DEFENCE OF THE ENLIGHTENMENT

Introductory Note

AFTER THE DEATH OF GOD AND THE COLLAPSE of utopias, on what intellectual and moral base do we want to build our communal life? If we are to conduct ourselves as responsible human beings, then we need a conceptual framework that underpins not only our statements – that is easy – but also our acts. Seeking just such a framework is what led me to a current of thought and sensibility that I will describe as the humanist dimension of the Enlightenment. The great upheaval that took place in the three-quarters of a century prior to 1789 is responsible more than anything else for our present-day identity. For the first time in history, human beings decided to take their destiny into their own hands and to set the welfare of humanity as the ultimate goal of their acts. This movement emanated from the whole of Europe, not just from one country alone, and it found expression in philosophy and in politics, in the sciences and in the arts, in novels and in autobiographies.

Clearly, a simple return to the past is neither possible nor desirable. The writers of the eighteenth century cannot resolve the problems that have arisen since and that are tearing apart our world every day. But a better understanding of this radical upheaval may help us live better today. And so I set out here to outline the key points of Enlightenment thought, without losing sight of our times, in a continual back-and-forth movement between past and present.

one

The Project

IT IS NOT EASY TO DEFINE EXACTLY WHAT THE Enlightenment project consisted in for two reasons. First, the Enlightenment was a period of culmination, recapitulation and synthesis, not one of radical innovation. The great ideas of the Enlightenment did not originate in the eighteenth century. Those that did not derive from Antiquity bear the traces of the High Middle Ages, the Renaissance and the classic era. The Enlightenment absorbed and articulated opinions that were in conflict until then, whence the need, as many historians have noted, to do away with certain commonplace images of it.

The Enlightenment was at once rationalist and empiricist, heir to Descartes and to Locke, receptive to the Ancients and to the Moderns, to the universalists and to the particularists, enamoured with history and eternity, details and abstractions, nature and art, freedom and equality. The ingredients were ancient but their combination was new. During the Age of Enlightenment, not only were these ingredients brought together to form a whole but, more essentially still, they were taken out of books and applied to the real world.

The second difficulty resides in the fact that Enlightenment thinking was formulated by a great many individuals who, far from agreeing with one another, were constantly engaged in bitter discussions, from one country to another and within each country. The time that has elapsed since has allowed us to put things in perspective but only to a certain point: some of those disagreements gave rise to schools of thought that are still in conflict today. The Enlightenment was an era of debate rather than consensus. Yet although the multiplicity of thought was considerable, we can recognize without too much difficulty what can be called an Enlightenment project.

Three ideas are found at the basis of this project, which

produce countless consequences of their own: autonomy; the human end purpose of our acts; and universality. What is to be understood by these ideas?

The first constitutive characteristic of Enlightenment thinking consists in giving priority to what individuals decide for themselves over what is imposed upon them by an external authority. This preference comprises two facets, one critical, the other constructive: it is necessary, on the one hand, to be free from external authorities and, on the other, to be guided by laws, norms and rules decided by the very people to whom they are addressed. *Emancipation* and *autonomy* are the words that designate these two equally indispensable phases of a single process. To engage in it, one must have total freedom to examine, question, criticize and challenge dogmas and institutions: none can be regarded as sacred. An indirect but decisive consequence of this preference is the restriction as to the character of authority: it must be on the same dimension as human beings, meaning it must be natural not supernatural. This is the sense in which the Enlightenment produced a 'disenchanted' world, obeying the same physical laws overall and, insofar as human societies were concerned, revealing the same mechanisms of behaviour.

Before the Enlightenment human beings lived, most of the time, under an authority that was religious in nature. Its origin was therefore both anterior to society (we speak, in this case, of 'heteronomy') and supernatural. Indeed, religion was the greatest target of Enlightenment criticism, the aim of which was to allow human beings to control their own destiny. However, this criticism was selectively directed. What was rejected was the submission of society and individuals to precepts whose sole legitimacy came from the fact that a tradition attributed them to gods or to ancestors; the lives of human beings were to be guided henceforth by a project for the future, not by an authority from the past. Nothing was said, on the other hand, about the religious experience per se, or about the idea of transcendence, or about any of the various moral doctrines propounded by particular religions. The criticism was aimed at the structure of society, not the content of beliefs. Religion was withdrawn from the realm of the state but not from the lives of individuals. The majority of Enlightenment thinkers identified not so much with atheism as with natural religion or deism, or one of the many variations thereof. When they undertook to observe and describe the beliefs of people around the world, they did so with the intent not of challenging religion but of fostering an attitude of tolerance and defending freedom of conscience.

Having cast off the shackles of the past, people set out to formulate new laws and norms using purely human means, without recourse this time to magic or revelation. The certainty of a unique source of light [*la lumière*] descended from above gave way to the idea of a plurality of light sources [*les lumières*] spreading from one person to another.[1] The first autonomy that needed to be acquired was that of knowledge. Hence the principle that no authority, no matter how well established and prestigious, is immune to criticism. Knowledge has two sources, reason and experience, and both are accessible to everyone. Reason was to be given priority as an instrument of knowledge, not as a motive for human conduct; it was opposed to faith, not to passions. Indeed, the latter were, in their turn, to be released from external constraints.

The emancipation of knowledge paved the way for the development of science. When people sought support from a prominent figure, they looked to scientists not philosophers, and so it was that Newton came to play a role in the Age of Enlightenment comparable to Darwin's

in subsequent centuries. Physics made spectacular progress, followed by the other sciences: chemistry, biology,
and even sociology and psychology. Champions of this
new thinking sought to bring the Enlightenment to all
because they were persuaded that it served the welfare of
all, the postulate being that knowledge liberates. Hence,
they promoted all forms of education, from primary
schools to scientific academies, and the dissemination of
knowledge, both in specialized publications and in ency-
clopaedias written for the general public.

The principle of autonomy caused an upheaval in the
life of the individual and that of societies. The fight for the
freedom of conscience that allows each person to choose
his or her religion was not new, but it had to be per-
petually renewed, and it was extended by the demand
for freedom of opinion, expression and publication.
Accepting human beings as the source of their own laws
means accepting them totally, as they are and not as they
ought to be. And the fact is that human beings are both
body and mind, passions and reason, sensuality and
meditation. It suffices to observe real people instead of
holding on to an abstract, idealized image of them to see
how infinitely diverse they are; this you can do by going

from one country to another, but also simply by looking from one individual to another. This idea was evidenced most tellingly not by scholarly texts but by the new genres that put the individual at the centre of attention: the novel, on the one hand, and the autobiography, on the other. These genres no longer aspired to reveal eternal laws of human conduct or the exemplary character of each gesture; they strove instead to show singular men and women in particular situations. This idea was also expressed in paintings that turned away from the great mythological and religious subjects to show the ordinary gestures of unexceptional human beings depicted in everyday activities.

The autonomy of individuals was extended to cover the environment in which they lived and the works they produced. In this way the natural environment was discovered to be made of forests and torrents, glades and hills unsubjected to geometrical or practical require- ments. At the same time, artists and their practices were granted a new role. Painters, musicians, actors and writers were no longer seen merely as entertainers or decorators, as simple servants to God, the king or a master. They became the exemplary embodiment of an appreciated activity: artists decided what they would create by themselves and they made their works for the purposes of sheer human enjoyment. The importance given to the natural environment and to works of art testified at the same time to the new dignity attributed to the sensible world.

The demand for autonomy transformed the political society even more deeply by broadening and consummating the separation between the temporal and the spiritual. In the Age of Enlightenment, this led first to a certain form of action, with authors communicating the results of independently conducted research of their own devising to benevolent rulers in the hope that the latter would alter their policies in consequence. This is what was expected of Frederick II in Berlin, Catherine II in St Petersburg and Joseph II in Vienna. But beyond the trend towards enlightened absolutism, which cultivated autonomy of reason in rulers but maintained the subjection of the people to their rule, the demand for autonomy led to two principles. The first was that of popular sovereignty, an old principle now given new content: the origin of political power was to be found in the people, and nothing was superior to the general will. The second was the principle of individual freedom vis-à-vis state power, legitimate or illegitimate, within the bounds of an individual sphere of action. To be defended, this freedom requires pluralism and a balance of powers. Everywhere, the separation between the theological and the political had to be imposed, with the latter organized from that point on on the basis of its own criteria.

There was a tendency for all sectors of society to become secular, even though people as individuals held on to their faith. This development was not only confined to political power. It concerned the legal system. From then on, only offences – that is, misdeeds against society – were punishable, and they were to be distinguished from sins – moral wrongdoing with respect to a tradition. It concerned education, destined to be taken out of the hands of ecclesiastical authorities as schools became places where enlightened ideas were taught, places open to all, and accordingly free, and at the same time compulsory for everyone. It concerned the press, where public debate had its place. And it concerned the economy, where arbitrary constraints had to be removed and the free circulation of goods permitted, and whose basis had to be the value of work and individual effort rather than the privileges and hierarchies of the past. The most suitable arena for all these changes to take place was the big city, where individual freedom was fostered and people had the chance to meet and discuss issues.

But once the will of the individual and the will of the community had been released from the oversight of earlier authorities, were they meant to be entirely free and without limits? No, the spirit of the Enlightenment cannot be reduced to this demand for autonomy alone, for it brought with it its own means of regulation. The first concerns the end purpose of freed human deeds, which was, in its turn, brought down to earth and focused on human beings rather than on God. In this sense the Enlightenment was a form of *humanism*, or, if one prefers, of anthropocentrism. It was no longer considered necessary, as theologians had maintained, to always be willing to sacrifice the love of creatures for the love of the Creator: it was henceforth enough to love other human beings. Whatever was waiting for us in the hereafter, human beings had to impart meaning to their earthly lives. The quest for salvation was replaced by the search for happiness. The state itself was there not to serve a divine plan but to assume responsibility for the welfare of its citizens. And the latter were not making a blame-worthy show of selfishness when they pursued happiness in the sphere of individual will, for they had every reason to treasure their private lives, to search for intensity of feelings and pleasures, and to cultivate affections and friendships.

The second restriction to the freedom of action of indi-viduals and communities consisted in asserting that all human beings by their very nature have inalienable rights. In this respect, the Enlightenment absorbed the heritage of the philosophy of natural right, as it was formulated in the seventeenth and eighteenth centuries. In addition to the rights that citizens enjoy within their society, they have others that are common to all human beings on earth, and although these rights may not be written down, they are no less imperious. Every human being has the right to life and hence the death penalty is illegitimate, even when it is applied to a criminal who has killed someone: if private murder is a crime, how can public murder not be? Every human being has the right to physical integrity and hence torture is illegitimate, even when it is practised for reasons of state. Belonging to the human race, to universal humanity, is more decisive than belonging to a specific society. The exercise of freedom was therefore contained by the principle of *universality*; and sacrality, which had broken free from dogmas and relics, finds embodiment in these newly recognized 'rights of man'.

If all human beings had a set of identical rights, it followed that they were equal before the law. The demand for equality followed from the principle of universality. And it opened the way to struggles for rights that continue to this day: women must be men's equals before the law; slavery must be abolished, since depriving a human being of freedom can never be legitimate; poor people, people with no position, and people on the margins of society must be recognized as having dignity too; and children are to be treated as individuals.

This affirmation of human universality aroused curiosity about foreign societies. Travellers and scholars did not from one day to the next stop judging people in distant cultures on the basis of criteria derived from their own cultures, but their interest had been awoken; they became aware of the manifold forms that civilization can assume and began to accumulate information and analyses that were to change their idea of humanity over time. The same reasoning was applied to temporal diversity: the past ceased to be regarded as the embodiment of an everlasting ideal or as a mere repertory of examples and came to be seen as a succession of historical periods, each with its own coherence and values. Knowledge of societies different from one's own enabled observers to direct a less naive gaze at themselves. In this way, Montesquieu could criticize the Persians, but also imagine the Persians judiciously criticizing the French.

These then are the broad outlines of the programme that was formulated in the Age of Enlightenment. How are we to judge it today, 250 years after its appearance? A twofold observation seems to be warranted. On the one hand, in Europe and everywhere in the world where the Enlightenment had an impact, it unquestionably came out victorious against the adversary it was fighting. Our knowledge of the world has progressed freely, without ideological prohibitions causing too much concern. Individuals do not fear the authority of tradition as much any more and try to manage their private space by themselves, enjoying all the while great freedom of expression. Democracy, where popular sovereignty is exercised with respect for individual liberties, has become a model that is cherished or desired everywhere. Universal human rights are considered a common ideal and equality before the law is the rule in any legitimate state. Pursuing personal happiness or common welfare are personal life choices that no longer shock anyone. This does not mean, of course, that these aims have been reached, but the ideal has been accepted and, still today, the existing order is criticized in terms inspired by the spirit of the Enlightenment. On the other hand, the anticipated benefits have not always been achieved and the promises formulated were not always kept. The twentieth century, in particular, which saw the bloodbath of the two world wars, totalitarian regimes established in Europe and elsewhere, and the deadly consequences of technological inventions, seemed to have definitively proven false all the hopes that had been formulated in the past, to the point that many people stopped claiming the Enlightenment as a reference and the ideas conveyed by such terms as humanism, emancipation, progress, reason and free will fell into disrepute.

The unrelieved distance between what could be seen as a promise and today's realities compels us to draw an initial conclusion: any strictly optimistic reading of history is illusory. And the fact is that faith in the linear, boundless progress of the human race tempted a number of Enlightenment thinkers. One of their most important precursors, the English poet Milton, regretted that humanity, obeying the dictates of tradition, wilfully stays in childhood, like a schoolboy who dares not move forward without instructions from his teacher. Milton expressed the hope that the free exercise of reason would one day enable humanity to enter adulthood. In France, Turgot gave a speech on the 'Successive Progress of the Human Spirit' (1750) in which he declared that 'morals become gentler, the human mind becomes more enlightened, isolated nations draw nearer to each other [...] the whole mass of the human race [...] advances continually, though slowly, towards greater perfection'.[2] (Admittedly, when he wrote these words, Turgot was only twenty-three!) Others, such as Voltaire and d'Alembert, engaged more or less cautiously on the same path. Lessing subscribed to the idea of progress in *The Education of the Human Race* (1780). Condorcet wrote a spiritual will from his hiding place during the persecutions brought on by the Terror (1793) and called it *Sketch for a Historical Picture of the Progress of the Human Mind.* All of these men believed that, no matter how slow and discontinuous such progress might be, humankind would eventually reach adulthood through the spread of culture and knowledge. This view of history as the accomplishment of a plan was picked up and reinforced by Hegel and then by Marx through whom it became part and parcel of the Communist doctrine.

It would be mistaken, however, to attribute this belief to the spirit of the Enlightenment itself. In point of fact, Turgot and Lessing's positions, for instance, were challenged at the time they were articulated. Many other thinkers, such as Hume and Mendelssohn, did not share their faith in a mechanical march to perfection, which is, by the way, nothing more than a transposition of the Christian doctrine on the ways of Providence into profane spaces; these men refused to read history as the accomplishment of a plan. The greatest French-language thinker of the Age of Enlightenment, Jean-Jacques Rousseau, stood in frontal opposition to this conception. He thought that the distinctive characteristic of the human species was not so much its march towards progress as its *perfectibility*, meaning its capacity to improve itself and the world – but the effects of this capacity were neither guaranteed nor irreversible. This attribute justified all efforts but did not ensure any success.

In addition, Rousseau believed that all progress was inevitably paid for by regression in another area. *Discourse on the Origin of Inequality* (1755) abounds in declarations to this effect: fortuitous causes 'have perfected human reason while deteriorating the species, made a being wicked while making him sociable'; 'all subsequent progress has been so many steps in appearance towards the perfection of the individual, and in effect towards the decrepitude of the species'; to the need 'to achieve distinction [...] we owe what is best and what is worst among men, our virtues and our vices'. Rousseau did not claim that deterioration was the only direction in which humankind was headed, nor did he recommend, as some would have it, a return to the past. He was, on the contrary, calling attention to the solidarity between positive and negative effects. The reason for this dual movement resides in the human condition itself. Human beings are endowed with the freedom that allows them to change themselves and the world, and it is this freedom that drives them to accomplish good and evil. It is perfectibility itself, at the source of man's greatest successes, that is responsible for his failures; this is the faculty that 'over the centuries, caus[ed] his enlightenment and his errors, his vices and his virtues to bloom'.[3] A distinctive characteristic of the human species is that people derive a sense of their own existence from the gaze of others, without which they cannot survive. This need manifests itself as much in love as in violence: the boys who throw petrol on girls who refuse their advances and then burn them act for this reason.[4] 'Good and evil flow from the same source,' Rousseau concludes.[5]

It follows that all hope of linear progress is vain. So-called 'social' problems are not temporary difficulties that a political party or a government could resolve through ingenious reforms once and for all: they are the consequence of our human condition. We can see today that Rousseau was right and that our aspiration to perfection does not imply faith in progress. Not only do technological and scientific advances not necessarily bring about moral and political improvements, but the advances themselves have nothing linear about them and can suddenly prove harmful. In undertaking to transform the world to make it conform to our need and desire, humankind often calls to mind the sorcerer's apprentice.

Agents of these transformations can predict their immediate effects but not the ultimate consequences occurring
decades if not centuries later. The example of atomic
fission is familiar to us all but it is almost too straightforward: the scientists who made this discovery could not
have imagined the horror of Hiroshima and Nagasaki,
but they sensed from the outset that there was reason for
concern about the use of their work. Does this mean that
the biologists working on the human genome should stop
their research because there might be a risk that the
results would be misused some time in the future? All
around us, our cars with their state-of-the-art engines
are producing toxic gases that contribute to upsetting the
planet's climate, and the machines that relieve us from
tiresome work consume more and more energy and cause
unemployment ... All conquests have a price.

The spirit of the Enlightenment applauded the
knowledge that releases human beings from oppressive
external authorities. But it did not consist in saying that,
everything being determined and knowable, people
would eventually learn how to wholly control the world
and shape it according to their desires. The complexity of
the matter is such that even the most ambitious scientific
hypotheses must always be formulated with a certain

amount of humility. 'Most effects come about by such singular ways and depend on causes so imperceptible and remote that they defy prediction,' Montesquieu writes in his *Treatise on Duties*.[6] This is even truer when it comes to the study of society, precisely because of the freedom of human beings to oppose their own nature and hence to act in unpredictable ways. 'Man, as a physical being, is like other bodies governed by invariable laws. As an intelligent being, he incessantly transgresses the laws established by God, and changes those of his own instituting.'[7] Knowledge of human societies comes up against the impossibility of predicting and controlling all the wills; the individual will comes up in turn against his or her inability to know the reasons for his or her own acts. What in the life of a human being is more important than the choice of a person to love? And yet neither will nor science succeeds in fully penetrating the secret of this choice. For this reason utopianism in any form, be it political or technical, is doomed to failure.

When we look today to Enlightenment thinking for support in dealing with our current difficulties, we cannot adopt unaltered the propositions formulated in the eighteenth century, not only because the world has changed, but also because the thinking was multiple, not one. Instead, what we need today is to re-establish Enlightenment thinking in a way that preserves the past heritage while subjecting it to a critical examination, lucidly assessing it in light of its wanted and unwanted consequences. In doing so, there is no risk that we will betray the Enlightenment. Just the opposite: it is through criticism that we remain faithful and put its teaching into practice.

two

Rejections and Distortions

FROM THE TIME OF ITS FORMULATION IN THE
eighteenth century, Enlightenment thinking was the
immediate object of much criticism. Its very principle was
sometimes rejected. As soon as the ideas were made
public, they spurred the predictable condemnation of the
ecclesiastical and civil authorities that were being challenged. Such reactions became even fiercer by the end of
the century in the wake of the political events that had
taken place in the interim. The Enlightenment came to be
equated with the Revolution and the Revolution with the
Terror, and this double equation led to condemning the

Enlightenment out of hand. 'The Revolution began with the Declaration of the Rights of Man,' asserted Louis de Bonald, one of its harshest opponents, 'which is why it ended in blood'.[8] The Enlightenment's mistake was to have replaced God as the source of ideals by man, collective traditions by reason (which each individual could use as he or she saw fit), hierarchy by equality, and unity by the cult of diversity.

Broadly speaking, the picture that Bonald and other conservatives of the Restoration era painted of the Enlightenment was correct: it was a fact that it gave pride of place to man, freedom and equality. What we are dealing with, in this case, is a head-on conflict, a fundamental disagreement about the principles and ideals of society, and so it is legitimate to speak here of a *rejection* of the Enlightenment. But often the situation was different. Criticisms of the Enlightenment frequently seemed to misread its spirit or more precisely to be addressed against a caricature thereof. And these caricatures or, to use a more neutral term, these distortions (*détournements*; in the eighteenth century the common term was 'corruptions') really existed. They too can be traced back to the time when Enlightenment ideas were first being

articulated. Some critics accused the Enlightenment
of going too far, others of not going far enough.
Montesquieu, for instance, was well aware that the very
principles he was championing could be harmful: he
warned against excessive recourse to reason and spoke of
the difficulties of freedom. He consequently compared
himself to someone living on the second floor who is
'disturbed by the noise upstairs and the smoke down-
stairs'. Rousseau for his part knew that when he had
finished battling the religious zealots, he would have to
contend with 'modern materialism'.[9] These distortions,
and not the Enlightenment itself, were what became most
often the object of rejection.

We have just seen a case in point. It was in the spirit of
the Enlightenment to posit the perfectibility of human
beings and of human societies. This idea was rejected
by those who thought that human beings had been
irremediably corrupted by the original sin. But the idea
could also be distorted, as when it was asserted that there
was a mechanical progress to human history; this view
simplified and rigidified the original idea while pushing
it to an extreme. When, in a counter movement, people
reject this doctrine of progress, citing a whole series of

examples to the contrary, they think they are rejecting the Enlightenment when, in actual fact, they are refuting one of its adversaries. Enlightenment thinking is this tight-rope act or, if you prefer, it is like a composition that is always played by a trio.

One of the common reproaches directed against the Enlightenment is that it provided the ideological founda-tions for late-nineteenth- and early-twentieth-century European colonialism. The reasoning runs as follows: the Enlightenment posited the unity of the human race and hence the universality of values; convinced that they stood for superior values, European states considered themselves authorized to bring their civilization to those less privileged than they and to guarantee the success of their enterprise; thus, they had to occupy the territories where these populations lived.

A specious look at the history of ideas might give the impression that Enlightenment thought paved the way for these later invasions. Condorcet was persuaded that civilized nations had the mission to bring light to all and that the 'European population [...] will sail to civilize or cause to disappear, even without conquest, those savage nations still occupying there immense tracts of country'.[10]

He dreamt of the establishment of a homogeneous universal state, and thought the intervention of the European nations could bring this about. It is also true that a hundred years later, ideologists of the French colonization legitimated their enterprise by arguing that, just as it is our duty to bring up our children, so it is our duty to help underdeveloped peoples. In 1874 economist and sociologist Paul Leroy-Beaulieu, an advocate of colonization, wrote: 'Colonization is within the social order the equivalent of not only reproduction but also education within the family.' It was an answer to a pressing need, he added years later (in 1891): 'We began to realize that about half the globe lived in a savage or barbarian state and solicited the methodical action and perseverance of civilized people.'[11] It was no accident that Jules Ferry, the French prime minister, an advocate of free mandatory education, became during the same period the great promoter of colonial conquests in Indochina and Africa. Such superior races as the French and the English have, he said, the duty to intervene in other countries, or, as he put it, 'the duty to civilize inferior races'.[12]

His words are not necessarily to be taken at face value, however. What they prove is that the Enlightenment enjoyed great prestige at the time and so those setting out on a perilous journey wanted it on their side. In the sixteenth century the Portuguese and Spanish did likewise when they used the obligation to spread Christianity to legitimate their conquests. But when the colonizers found themselves obliged to defend their actions step by step, they quickly dropped their humanitarian arguments. Maréchal Bugeaud, conqueror of Algeria in the mid-nineteenth century, made no pretence about his aims when he assumed responsibility before the French National Assembly for the massacres of Algerians. 'I have always given preference to French interests over some absurd philanthropy for foreigners who cut off the heads of our imprisoned or wounded soldiers.'[13] In a speech to the same Assembly, Tocqueville, then a deputy, agreed that Bugeaud's 'main merit was not exactly that of being a philanthropist [...] but what I do believe is that Monsieur le Maréchal Bugeaud did great service to his country in Africa'.[14]

When Jules Ferry was cornered by his opponents in the National Assembly who accused him of betraying the principles of the Enlightenment, he abandoned his ground, claiming that the theory of a civilizing mission 'belongs neither to politics nor to history, but to political metaphysics'.[15] The politics of colonization were camouflaged behind Enlightenment ideals, but in reality they were driven by straightforward national interests. And nationalism was not a product of the Enlightenment; the most one can say is that it is a distortion thereof, insofar as it recognizes no limit to popular sovereignty. The anti-colonialist movements were, in this respect, much more directly inspired by the principles of the Enlightenment, in particular when they posited human universality, equality between peoples and individual freedom. Colonization in the nineteenth and twentieth centuries had this surprising and potentially self-destructive characteristic: it brought with it the Enlightenment ideas from which its enemies drew inspiration.

Another particularly serious reproach directed against the spirit of the Enlightenment is that it unwittingly produced the totalitarian regimes of the twentieth century, with their procession of exterminations, imprisonments and sufferings inflicted upon millions of people. The argument runs something like this: having rejected God, human beings define their own criteria of good and evil, and intoxicated by their ability to understand the world, they try to reshape it to conform to their ideals; in so doing, they do not hesitate to eliminate or reduce to slavery sizeable portions of the earth's population. This critique of the Enlightenment was formulated notably by a number of Christian authors, belonging to different denominations. It can be found expressed by T. S. Eliot, an Anglican, in a short book written in 1939 entitled *The Idea of a Christian Society*; by Aleksandr Solzhenitsyn, a Russian Orthodox, in his 1978 Harvard speech; or yet again by Pope John Paul II, particularly in the last book finished before he died, *Memory and Identity*.

Writing at the beginning of World War II and more precisely at the onset of the war between Great Britain and Germany, Eliot sought to demonstrate that the only true opposition to totalitarianism could come from an authentically Christian society. 'If you will not have God (and He is a jealous God) you should pay your respects to Hitler or Stalin,'[16] he concluded, seeing the rejection of God as the outcome of the Enlightenment that made it possible to establish modern states on purely human foundations. Solzhenitsyn's reproach in his Harvard address is even more emphatic. At the root of totalitarianism is 'the prevailing Western view of the world which was first born during the Renaissance and found its political expression from the period of the Enlightenment. It became the basis for government and social science and could be defined as rationalistic humanism or humanistic autonomy: the proclaimed and enforced autonomy of man from any higher force above him. It could also be called anthropocentricity, with man seen as the centre of everything that exists.' But if one automatically leads to the other, then is it not time to change ideals? 'It would be retrogression to attach oneself today to the ossified formulas of the Enlightenment,' Solzhenitsyn concludes.[17]

The genealogy that John Paul II outlines is not very different. The 'evil ideologies' at work in totalitarianism derive from the history of European philosophy, from the Renaissance, Cartesianism and the Enlightenment. The mistake of this line of thought was to replace the search for salvation by the pursuit of happiness. 'Man remained alone: alone as creator of his own history and his own civilization; alone as one who decides what is good and what is bad.' It is just a step from here to the gas chambers. 'If man can decide by himself, without God, what is good and what is bad, he can also determine that a group of people is to be annihilated.' By rejecting Christ, the European Enlightenment 'paved the way for the great historical catastrophes of the twentieth century'.[18]

In this view of history, the difference between totalitarian and democratic states is blurred, since both have their common root in the Enlightenment. For Eliot, this difference is of secondary importance, since both participate in the same atheism, individualism and infatuation with material objects alone. For Solzhenitsyn, they are variations on the same model: 'In the East, [spiritual life] is destroyed by the dealings and machinations of the ruling party. In the West, commercial interests tend to suffocate it. This is the real crisis. The split in the world is less terrible than the similarity of the disease plaguing its main sections.'[19] John Paul II regards the moral permissiveness that characterizes Western societies as 'another form of totalitarianism, subtly concealed under the appearances of democracy'. Totalitarian Marxism and Western liberalism are barely distinguishable variations on the same ideology, the product of the aspiration to material success alone. And 'when a parliament authorizes the termination of pregnancy, agreeing to the elimination of the unborn child',[20] it does not act very differently from that other parliament that delegated full powers to Hitler and paved the way to the 'final solution'.

There is a need for us to distinguish here between the different types of accusations brought against the Enlightenment. To begin with, a prestigious ideology can serve as a camouflage, as we have seen for colonialism. Unlike Nazism, Communism claimed this glorious heritage as its own but only in its grandiloquent programmes. One would have been hard put to find any traces of the heritage in the actual workings of Communist societies: individual autonomy was reduced to nothing, the principle of equality was belied by the omnipresence of unchanging hierarchies within the governing class, the search for knowledge was subjected to ideological dogmas (genetics and relativity theory were bourgeois doctrines that needed to be repressed), and the 'humanism' of manifestos was but a mirage. Rather than devote themselves to the pursuit of personal happiness, people were obliged to sacrifice themselves on the altar of some remote collective salvation. Material values were far from victorious: Communism had the greatest difficulty in producing a society of bounty. In truth, it constituted something of a political religion, and this is far removed from the spirit of the Enlightenment and of democracy.

Alongside this purely decorative use of the Enlightenment, Communism utilized it in other ways that correspond to distortions. Condemning them, this time, is perfectly legitimate, but the judgement is not really directed against the Enlightenment, where primacy was given to autonomy, knowledge was wrested from the control of morality, and the search for truth from the imperatives of virtue. In Communism, an inflated appetite for the autonomy of knowledge was pushed to such an extreme that knowledge could pretend to produce values. And indeed, such scientism was used by totalitarian regimes in the twentieth century to justify their violence. On the pretext that the laws of history, as revealed by science, spelled the end of the bourgeoisie, Communism did not hesitate to exterminate the members of this class. On the pretext that the laws of biology, as revealed by science, demonstrated the inferiority of certain 'races', the Nazis put to death those whom they identified as their members. In democratic states, these forms of violence are inconceivable, but the authority of science is nonetheless cited to legitimate choices, as if the values of a society could follow automatically from knowledge. Scientism is dangerous, to be sure, but it cannot be deduced from the spirit of the Enlightenment because the Enlightenment, as we have seen, rejects the idea that the world is totally transparent to the eye of the scientist and that the ideal proceeds from a straightforward observation of the world (what should be from what is). Scientism is a distortion of the Enlightenment, its enemy not its avatar.

Finally, there are certain characteristics of the spirit of the Enlightenment cited by Eliot, Solzhenitsyn, John Paul II and other critics that do correspond to its identity — namely, autonomy, anthropocentrism, a vision of politics and morality based on purely human foundations, and the preference for arguments based on reason over arguments based on authority. In this case, what is being rejected is real enough but is the rejection well founded? John Paul II accuses the morality that resulted from the Enlightenment of being purely subjective, depending on will alone, and susceptible to pressure from those in power, unlike Christian morality, which he deems immutable because it is objectively based on God's word. There is reason to wonder whether the latter's objectivity is real since no one can claim direct contact with God, and people are obliged to put themselves in the hands of intermediaries, accredited by purely human agencies, prophets and theologians who claim to know the divine plan. The orthodoxy of a religion depends on a group of human beings who have handed a tradition down to us. The morality of the Enlightenment is *inter-subjective*, not subjective; the principles of good and evil are the subject of a consensus; this consensus is potentially that of all of humanity, and it is established through an exchange of rational arguments, which are consequently founded on a universal human character-istic. The morality of the Enlightenment proceeds not from egotistical self-love but from respect for humankind.

Whether you regret it or not, the Enlightenment conception of justice is less revolutionary than its critics suggest. The law is, of course, the expression of the autonomous will of the people, but this will is restrained within limits. True to the Ancients, Montesquieu declares that justice is anterior and superior to laws. 'Justice is not dependent on human laws,' he writes in *Treatise on Duties*, 'it is founded on the existence and sociability of reasonable beings, and not on the dispositions or particular wills of those beings.' And in *The Spirit of Laws*, 'To say that there is nothing just or unjust but what is commanded or forbidden by positive laws, is the same as saying that before the describing of a circle all the radii were not equal.'[21] The laws persecuting the bourgeois and the kulaks in Russia, or the Jews and the Roms in Germany, contravened the principles of justice. Not only do these principles enjoy a broad consensus (people will not readily accept that a part of the population has to be exterminated for the benefit of another), they are written in the constitution (or in the preamble to the constitution) of most democratic countries. The will of the people is autonomous; it is not arbitrary.

The different forms of rejection and distortion of the Enlightenment cannot be conflated and the same arguments cannot be deployed to fight them. What has changed is their relative importance: the adversary who leaned on the heritage of the Enlightenment was not as threatening in the past as those who criticized it from the outside; the opposite is true today. Yet, both dangers are still present, and it is not an accident that those who uphold the spirit of the Enlightenment find themselves defending it on both fronts. In this way, an organization for the defence of women has chosen to define itself as neither this nor that, '*Ni putes ni soumises*', 'neither whores nor submissives'.[22] To treat women as submissives is to reject the spirit of the Enlightenment; to reduce them to whores is to distort their demand for freedom. It is not because we refuse one road that we have to embrace the other: the road of autonomy, humanism and universality also remains open.

Now let us take a closer look at a few of these debates.

three

Autonomy

A TWOFOLD MOVEMENT IS FOUND AT THE POINT
of departure of the upheaval caused by Enlightenment
thinking: a negative movement of liberation from norms
imposed from the outside and a positive movement of
construction of new norms of our own devising. The good
citizen, Rousseau wrote, knows how to 'act according to
the maxims of his own judgement'. In a contemporary
article in the *Encyclopédie*, Diderot sketched the portrait
of his ideal hero, 'a philosopher who, by riding rough-
shod over prejudice, tradition, antiquity, universal
consent, authority, in a word, everything that subjugates

the mass of minds, dares to think for himself'.[23] This philosopher refuses to submit to any master without discussion and always prefers to base his thoughts on what is accessible to everyone: evidence from the senses and the capacity to reason. At the end of the century, Kant confirmed that the first principle of the Enlightenment resided in upholding autonomy: 'Have the courage to use your own understanding, is thus the motto of the Enlightenment'; 'the maxim of thinking for oneself at all times is enlightenment'.[24]

All facts, Diderot argued, 'are equally subject to criticism'. In the moral and political sciences, Condorcet insisted, 'We must have the courage to examine everything, to discuss everything, even to teach everything.' And Kant concluded, 'Our age is the age of criticism, to which everything must be subjected.'[25] This did not mean that human beings could do without tradition, that is, without a heritage transmitted by their elders. Living in a culture is the natural state for human beings and the fact is that culture and, to begin with, language are transmitted by those who came before us. Imagining that we can reason without prejudices is the worst form of prejudice. Tradition is constitutive of human beings; it is simply that it does not suffice to make a principle legitimate or a proposition true.

Such a stance had obvious political consequences. A people is made up of individuals, and if they start thinking for themselves, they will want to take their destiny into their own hands. The question of the origin and legitimacy of the political was not new. Two principal interpretations were pitted against each other in the eighteenth century. Some saw the king as receiving his crown from God, no matter how many intermediaries there may have been between the source and the final beneficiary; and, as a divine right monarch, he could not be held accountable by anyone on earth. According to others, who called on reason, nature or an original contract, the source of power was in the people, in common law and in general interest, for God had created human beings free and endowed them with reason. 'Every man who is supposed a free agent, ought to be his own governor,' Montesquieu maintained.[26] This did not mean that the king should be overthrown. The prevailing opinion at the time was that the people had placed the power in the hands of the prince because their multiplicity prevented them from governing themselves. The latter ruled beyond appeal but not irresponsibly for his reign was meant to serve the interests of his country.

It was against this backdrop that Rousseau expounded his radical ideas in *The Social Contract*. Not only did he defend the human origin of all power against its divine origin, he declared that this power could not be transmitted, that it could only be confided, as one would entrust a task to a servant. This power was, in Rousseau's words, inalienable. What the people gave to the government for a moment could always be taken back. Common interest, the only source of legitimacy, was expressed in what Rousseau called the general will. This was translated in turn into laws. '[L]egislative power belongs to the people'; if a state that is regulated by laws is a republic, then 'all lawful governments are republican'.[27] According to Rousseau, the people had forgotten that this power belonged to them, even when exercised by the king, and that they could take it back at any time. Some years later, a group of men in a British colony drew the necessary conclusions from this reasoning and declared their right to freely choose their own government. Thus the first modern republic in Rousseau's sense was born and called the United States of America. A few years after that, the same ideas were posited by the leading actors in the French Revolution.

Freedom for the people was accompanied by autonomy for individuals. They engaged in knowledge without bowing to earlier authorities, freely chose their religion, expressed their ideas in public, and organized their private lives as they saw fit. It would be a mistake to assume that the demand by Enlightenment thinkers that experience and reason be given priority over traditions translated into a hypothesis on the nature of human beings: they knew perfectly well that our species is not reasonable. 'Reason is, and ought only to be the slave of the passions,' Hume declared, before noting that reason is not always used wisely: 'It is not contrary to reason to prefer the destruction of the whole world to the scratching of my finger.'[28] Reason is an instrument that can serve indifferently good and evil; criminals make use of great powers of reason to commit crimes! Human beings are driven by their will and their desires, by their affections and their conscience, and also by forces over which they have no control; nevertheless, reason can enlighten them in their search for truth and justice.

Autonomy is a good thing, but autonomy does not

mean self-sufficiency. Human beings are born, live and die in societies; without them, they would not be human. It is the gaze of others that is the source of the child's consciousness, and it is the call of others that awakens language. The feeling of existence, which no one can do without, derives from interaction with others. All human beings suffer from congenital insufficiency, from a sense of incompleteness that they try to fill by attaching themselves to those around them and soliciting their attachment. Rousseau was once again the theorist who most forcefully expressed this need, and his testimony is all the more precious insofar as he was personally ill at ease with others and preferred getting away from them. But solitude is still a form of this communal life that it is neither possible nor desirable to leave. 'Our sweetest existence is relative and collective, and our true *self* is not entirely within us. Finally, such is man's constitution in this life that one never is able to enjoy oneself well without the co-operation of another.'[29] This does not mean that life in society is necessarily good; Rousseau was continually warning against the alienation of the self that results from the pressures of fashion and common opinion and concern about what others will think. When people live only in the eyes of others, they neglect their inner being and devote themselves to appearances alone; and public display becomes their unique aim. The 'desire for a reputation', the 'ardour to be talked about', 'the frenzy to achieve distinction'[30] become the main motives for acts, and these become increasingly conformist and meaningless.

No sooner had this idea been formulated than a distortion of it emerged. It is found in the writings of the Marquis de Sade, who proclaimed that solitude expressed the truth of the human being. 'Are we not all born solitary, isolated? I say more: are we not all come into the world enemies, the one of the other, all in a state of perpetual and reciprocal warfare?'[31] From this initial state of solitude, Sade inferred the need for self-sufficiency as a rule of life: the only thing that counts is my pleasure and I need to take others into consideration only to protect myself against their intrusions. How can we not see that these statements run against not only the spirit of the Enlightenment but also common sense? Who has ever seen a child born isolated (without a mother) and, especially, survive alone in the world? Humans are even the animal species whose young ones are the slowest to acquire a minimal degree of independence: the abandoned child will die from lack of care, not from the effect of 'perpetual and reciprocal warfare'. This long period of vulnerability may be precisely what is at the root of the feeling of compassion that is familiar to all human beings.

Sade's statements, despite their implausibility, were well received in the centuries that followed as writers picked up in chorus the idea that human beings are fundamentally and essentially alone (to the point that one wonders if they ever saw a child being born or growing up)? To take just two examples, Maurice Blanchot in an essay on Sade and Georges Bataille in *Eroticism* saw Sade's great merit in this idea. According to Blanchot, Sade's morality is 'founded on the primary fact of absolute solitude. Sade said it and repeated it in all its forms: nature creates us alone; there is no connection whatsoever linking one man to another [...] The true man knows he is alone and he accepts this.'[32] Bataille quotes these lines from Blanchot and agrees that 'the solitary man for whom he speaks pays not the slightest heed to his fellows'. For this reason, Bataille adds, we have to be grateful to Sade who 'gave us a true-to-life picture of the man for whom the other no longer matters'.[33]

Individual sovereignty, according to Bataille's reading of Sade, would be expressed precisely in the negation of any subject other than oneself. 'Solidarity with everybody else prevents a man from having the sovereign attitude.'[34] Caring for others can only result from the fear of fully coming to terms with oneself. According to Blanchot, the 'true man' 'renounces everything within himself that exists only in relationship to others, to a tradition of seventeen centuries of cowardliness'.[35] Individual autonomy is taken here to such an extreme that it destroys itself, conflated as it is with the negation of others and hence ultimately with self-negation.

When the two demands for collective autonomy and individual autonomy were first formulated, their proponents did not imagine that a conflict could arise between the two. People's sovereignty was conceived on the model of individual freedom, and so the relationship was regarded as one of continuity. Condorcet was the first to point out the danger. As an elected representative to the Legislative Assembly, he was in a good position to observe eventual abuses of power. Examining problems of public education, he warned against the undue encroachment of collective authority on the sphere of individual freedom.

According to Condorcet, schools must abstain from ideological indoctrination. 'Freedom of opinion would be but
an illusion if society were to take hold of new generations
to dictate to them what they must believe.' Such teaching,
which pupils would be unable to evaluate by themselves
or contest, would inculcate 'prejudices' and it is not
because these prejudices proceed from popular will that
they are any less tyrannical. This type of instruction
would represent 'an attack against one of the most
precious aspects of natural freedom'. For this reason it is
necessary to remove a sphere from the control of public
power, and thereby preserve the critical faculty of
individuals. 'The goal of instruction is not to make men
admire a ready-made legislation, but to render them
capable of assessing it and correcting it.'[36]

Today, we are in a position to fully appreciate the
clear-sightedness of Condorcet's description of the way
in which totalitarian powers were to oppress their populations in the twentieth century (I will come back to this
later). Since the fall of these regimes, we have seen the
possibility of a distortion of the Enlightenment in the
opposite direction, the consequences of which are
disturbing in their turn. On the one hand, states can

deprive the inhabitants of the country of their freedom; on the other, particularly powerful individuals can restrain popular sovereignty. In this case, the danger comes not so much from dictators as from a few people with substantial financial means.

Let us take two examples of this loss of popular sovereignty linked to international relations. The first has to do with economic globalization. Nowadays, states can defend their borders with weapons if need be but they are no longer able to arrest the flow of capital. As a result, a person or a group of people with no political legitimacy whatsoever can decide whether or not to transfer their capital elsewhere and with a click of the mouse plunge a country into unemployment or avoid immediate catastrophe, provoke social disturbances or help to avert them. The successive governments in a country like France would have been delighted to lower unemployment: they may no longer have the means to do so. Control of the economy is no longer a matter of popular sovereignty: regardless of what we think of it, we cannot fail to see the limits imposed on political autonomy.

The second example is in another sphere altogether: that of international terrorism. Recent terrorist attacks were perpetrated not by states conducting aggressive policies but by individuals or groups of individuals. In the past, only a state, and only the most powerful, could organize such complex strikes as those carried out in New York, Istanbul, Madrid and London, which were the work of a few dozen people. Technological advances have made the manufacture of dangerous weapons accessible to groups of individuals. These weapons have become less and less expensive and their miniaturization has made them easier to transport. All you need is a cellphone to trigger an explosion. In this way, one of the most common everyday objects can be used as a formidable weapon! It is relatively easy for perpetrators of such acts to hide and escape military retaliation, for an individual has no territory. They come from several countries but identify with none: they are stateless. Modern states are poorly equipped to fight against this other form of globalization, which is equally destructive of their sovereignty.

There is also an erosion of autonomy from within these states, the source of which is not so much state power as diffuse forces that are hard to pinpoint. Aside from the oppression exerted by the economic machine, which assumes the impersonal form of fatality and prevents individuals from implementing their will (what can one person alone do to fight against unemployment?), other forces are no less paralysing. We think we are making up our own minds, but if the media repeat the same message day in and day out, what leeway do we have to form our own opinions? Mass media – print, radio and especially the television – are omnipresent, and the fact is that decisions are based on the news that is available to us. Even when the information we receive is not false, it has been selected, sorted and arranged to lead us to one conclusion rather than another. Media organs do not express the collective will and this is not something to regret: individuals should be able to judge for themselves and not under the pressure of decisions made by the state. Unfortunately, nothing guarantees the impartiality of the news.

In certain countries, if you have a lot of money, you can buy a television station or even five or ten of them plus radio stations and newspapers, and have them say what you like so that viewers, listeners and readers will think what you like. In this case, what we have is a plutocracy not a democracy: it is money not the people who have power.

Elsewhere, it is not so much a matter of money as of the influence of fashion and the spirit of the age or of the place. The journalists are not controlled by the state or by money and yet they all agree wholeheartedly: they follow the lead of those with the greatest reputations, afraid to seem out of phase, and they pursue an identical mission. The phenomenon is not new, but in a world of around-the-clock news, it has gained tremendous momentum. The Internet, where information is emitted by uncontrolled individuals and made accessible to all, generated what may very well be vain hopes. There is no control over the information, be it accurate or manipulated, and nothing enables the average layperson to distinguish one from the other.

If it is very powerful, public opinion can restrict individual freedom, which ends up yielding to it. Rousseau was very attentive to this dimension of modern societies; for this reason, he recommended raising children in relative solitude, far from the pressures of fashion and *idées reçues*; for the same reason, he preferred living far from big cities. In his day already, this solution could have seemed utopian. Since then, the world has gone in the opposite direction. Mass-media, and notably television, have penetrated into private space as much in the city as in the country: children in particular can spend hours in front of the TV screen every day. Television is not subject to state control but it needs money to function; this comes from commercials, in other words from sellers of consumable goods. Through advertising, but also through the lifestyles that it shows in programmes and news reports, the television medium provides us with a model to imitate, without ever explicitly formulating it — which makes it all the more difficult to challenge.

Enlightenment thinking fosters the development of a critical spirit. This principle still needs to be defended today, notably against those who react to any criticism that displeases them by immediately taking the matter to court. Freedom of opinion must be protected, and this includes opinions that disturb us. This does not mean that a critical stance is admirable in and of itself. Those who, benefiting from the freedom of expression that exists in the democratic public space, adopt an attitude of wholesale denigration, turn criticism into a pointless game that subverts their own starting point. Too much criticism kills criticism. In the Enlightenment tradition, criticism represented the first step in a dual movement to be followed by reconstruction. In his *Memoirs*, Raymond Aron relates a formative anecdote from his youth when, alarmed at the rise of Nazism in Germany in the thirties, he outspokenly criticized the attitude of the French government. Having listened to him attentively, a French minister offered to transmit his criticism to the president of the Council of State, but first he asked Aron to take another step and answer the question, 'What would you do if you were in his place?'[37] Because he understood this lesson, Aron became an intellectual who stood apart. Without a positive counterpart, critical discourse leads nowhere. Indiscriminate scepticism and systematic mockery have only an appearance of wisdom; by distorting the spirit of the Enlightenment, they create a solid obstacle to its action.

four

Secularism

ROYAL POWER ESTABLISHED BY DIVINE RIGHT was not the only thing that threatened the autonomy of society, which represents a complex aggregate of conflicting forces. Since the beginnings of European history we have grown accustomed to distinguishing between temporal and spiritual power. When each enjoys autonomy in its sphere and is protected against the encroachment of the other, we speak of a *secular* society.

One may have thought that the relations between the two would be straightforward in the areas of the world marked by the Christian tradition, since Christ announced that his kingdom was not of this world and that submission to God in no way interferes with submission to Caesar. Yet from the moment that Constantine imposed Christianity as a state religion in the fourth century, the temptation emerged to seize all power. The reason for this is easy to understand. The temporal order governs the body, and the spiritual order governs the soul, but body and soul are not simply juxtaposed entities; they inevitably form a hierarchy within each individual. For the Christian religion, the soul must rule over the body. It follows therefore that it is incumbent upon religious institutions – that is to say, the Church – not only directly to govern the soul but also indirectly to control the body, and hence the temporal realm. The temporal authority in its turn seeks to defend its prerogatives and maintain control over all worldly matters, which means over an institution like the Church as well. To protect its autonomy, each of the two adversaries is tempted to encroach upon the realm of the other.

In 754, to justify their ambitions, advocates of unlimited spiritual power issued a forgery that was destined to play a major role in this conflict. *The Donation of Constantine* claimed that the first Christian emperor had entrusted to the papacy not only the care of the souls of the faithful but also sovereignty over all the lands of Western Europe. In the latter half of the twelfth century, under Pope Alexander III, these pretensions were codified in the doctrine known as *plenitudo potestatis*, or 'fullness of power'. According to this doctrine, whereas the pope held the authority of two symbolic swords, the spiritual and the temporal, the emperor held only the latter, and therefore the pope was the emperor's hierarchic superior.

This is the project of a *theocracy*, the first form of fullness of power, whereby the temporal authority is simply put into the service of the religious project. In opposition to this, a wholly different form developed at the same time, one that aspired to turn the Church into an instrument among others in the service of the temporal authority. The most forceful emperors embodied this attitude (which was already Constantine's). This is sometimes called *caesaropapism*. In its diverse forms, it opposes theocracy but not the aspiration to fullness of power. Whether the state is put into the service of the Church or vice versa, each wants to have full power. Only the impossibility of achieving a decisive victory led to the limitation of each force by its rival. Civil power and ecclesiastical power co-existed throughout the period we call the Middle Ages, and the boundary between them was merely the line where the last battle ended. Each reigned absolutely in its realm. Individuals, for their part, had no freedom of choice.

The terms of the debate shifted after the Reformation, because of the place that the latter reserved for the individual. A simple peasant who could speak to God could be right and the pope wrong; after all, the latter was not immune to heresy. The temporal sovereign, Luther thought at first, must respect the inviolable realm of what theologians call 'immanent acts', that is to say, the relationship to God, the inner life and the conscience. The prince had no rival in the exercise of his power, but his power was limited, not so much by the power of the Church as by the conscience of the individual, who is answerable to God alone. A third force had emerged here, interfering with the prior opposition between temporal power and spiritual power − namely the individual, who was alone responsible for his communication with God and who would soon take charge of other areas wrenched from the control of the old powers. At the outset, then, the individual was but the name for the framework within which religious experience could be safeguarded against intrusions from political authorities. This individual framework was eventually expanded, whereupon it needed to be defended not only against the state but also against ecclesiastical authorities. This is the meaning of modern secularism.

Modern European history from the Renaissance to the Enlightenment, from Erasmus to Rousseau, is the history of the strengthening of the separation between public institutions and religious traditions, and the growth of individual freedom. Indeed, the Church's temporal power was shaken without being abolished, as the many steps taken in favour of religious tolerance demonstrate. And so Rousseau had cause to protest in a letter to Voltaire in 1756, 'I am outraged, as you are, that the faith of everyone is not in the most perfect liberty, and that man dares control the interior of consciences, where he ought not to penetrate.'[38]

One after another, entire segments of society called for the elimination of religious supervision and the right to autonomy. One of the most significant demands was made by Cesare Beccaria in *An Essay on Crimes and Punishments* (published when he was twenty-six), wherein he clearly set forth the distinction between sins and crimes, which made it possible to remove legislative acts from the religious context. Laws pertain only to relationships between humans in the polity and transgressing them has nothing to do with religious doctrine. Sins, on the other hand, do not constitute statutory offences. In this way law and theology were no longer conflated.

Beccaria noted another threat to individual freedom, this time not from the Church (which must not have temporal power) or from the state (which must not interfere with spiritual matters) but from the family. In families, the head can exercise a form of tyranny over the other members and hence deprive them of the independence acquired with regard to social structures. Just as each individual having reached the age of reason had the right to address God directly, so he could also appeal directly to the republic of which he is a member to benefit from the rights that it guarantees. Then 'the spirit of liberty will not only breathe in each public place of the city, and in the assemblies of the nation, but in private houses where men find the greatest part of their happiness and misery'.[39]

In a modern liberal democracy, the individual's

conduct is therefore divided not so much between two realms, the temporal and the spiritual, as between three. At one end is the private and personal realm; here the individual is alone responsible and nobody else has any say in these matters. From the time of the Reformation, freedom of conscience was expanded to encompass all private acts. At the other end is the legal realm where the individual is subject to strict norms guaranteed by the state: these he cannot transgress without becoming a criminal. Between the two is a vast public or social area steeped in norms and values, which are not, however, binding. Whereas in the legal realm orders are pronounced and punishments imposed, here advice is given and disapproval expressed in the context of a public debate: this, then, is the realm of moral rules, pressures exerted by fashion, the spirit of the age and religious prescriptions (therefore it is the former realm of spiritual power).

The map of these three areas varies from country to country and from one historical period to another but the need to distinguish between them and set their boundaries is recognized by all. For our contemporaries, secularism consists in the fact that each remains master of his or her own house as long as that individual does not encroach upon others. The state controls the legal sphere but cannot impose its will on civil society; and civil society occupies the public sphere but cannot extend its reach beyond the confines where individual freedom is protected. In addition, the state guarantees the freedom and protection of individuals in relation to civil society. This balance between areas may be fragile (witness, for instance, the debate on abortion) but it is indispensable for the good working of the community. Maintaining this balance is one of the state's responsibilities.

Now let's come back to a point already mentioned, namely Condorcet's discovery at the time of the French Revolution of a new danger for individual autonomy and hence for the secularism of society. This danger consisted in the fact that those who held temporal power aspired less to subjugate an existing religion (the intent of caesaropapism) than to found a new cult around the state itself, its institutions or its representatives. That it became apparent to Condorcet at the time was because it was non-existent beforehand, since the presence of an official religion prevented temporal powers from becoming one. The removal of the Christian Church from its dominant position is what made this new religion possible. The very same people who strove to free men from the shackles of religion risked becoming the servants of a no less oppressive cult. When ruling powers dictate to people what they should think, then we are dealing with 'a kind of political religion' that is hardly preferable to the one it replaced. To Condorcet, 'Robespierre is a priest and never will be anything else.'[40] This is the first known occurrence of the expression 'political religion', a concept very different from Rousseau's 'civil religion', which simply involved recognizing the principles of communal life.

Ultimately, the specific content of the new dogma mattered little. It could be a question of civic moralism, as in the dreams of certain revolutionaries to rebuild ancient Sparta, or, to the contrary, of mercantilism, a pure search for profit, which made the exploitation of slaves or the subjugation of foreign populations lawful. What mattered was the new 'fullness of power' since temporal power also imposed the beliefs that it thought best for it. By its control over education, it transformed instruction – theoretically liberating – into an instrument of greater subjugation; it presented its political decisions as immutable dogmas or, worse, as scientific truths. By its control over the news, it could make sure that 'the citizens never learn anything that is not appropriate to confirm them in the opinions their masters have wished to inspire in them'.[41] Manipulated in this way, people think they're acting freely, when they are actually executing the programme conceived by the ruling power.

Condorcet unfolds before the reader's eyes a real doomsday scenario. Imagine, he says, that 'a troop of audacious hypocrites' manages to get control of the central power in a country and to create relays throughout its regions. It could lay its hands on the main sources of information and consequently be believed by 'a people whose ignorance makes them prey to the phantoms of fear'. Alternating seduction and threats, it 'will exercise under the mask of liberty'[42] a tyranny that is in no way less efficient than those that preceded it.

Such fullness of powers would even be worse than earlier forms, since the area covered by the new political religion is conflated with man's entire worldly existence. Traditional religion sought to control the individual's conscience, either by exercising temporal power directly, or by delegating the task of constraint to the latter. Political religion, on the other hand, could directly oversee and govern everything. As a result, the freedom that Condorcet advocated was not only freedom of conscience; as Benjamin Constant, an attentive reader of Condorcet's *Mémoires*, noted fifteen years later, it was all of the freedom of the Moderns. Indeed, the Ancients did not conceive of freedom in these terms; they did not imagine that the individual needed to be defended against his own representatives. The territory of the new religion exceeds by far that of the old and consequently the territory that the citizen has to defend is that much greater.

The Jacobin Terror already embodied a first form of 'political religion'. But it was not until 130 years later, at the beginning of the twentieth century, that Condorcet's worst fears were to come true, with the rise in Europe in the wake of World War I of several political regimes that corresponded to his premonitory image: Communism, Nazism and fascism. In all likelihood, Condorcet's statements had been forgotten by that time, yet already in the twenties a number of attentive observers discerned the characteristics of what they in their turn called a political religion. Among these observers, who ran the gamut from Catholic Italian and German journalists to authors of seminal works like Eric Voegelin or of brilliant articles like Raymond Aron's, particular mention should be made of Waldemar Gurian, a Russian Jew converted to Catholicism, who lived in Germany before emigrating to Switzerland and later to the United States and who was already writing comparative studies of European totalitarianism in the twenties.

Both Gurian and these other observers noted the paradox of using the term 'religion' for a doctrine that stood out clearly against traditional confessions and that, in the case of Communism, virulently opposed it. For this reason he proposed to borrow the term 'ideocracy' from the contemporary movement of Eurasians, Russian emigrants animated by an anti-European spirit, and to include in it two sub-categories: traditional religions and the new political religions. The distinction between the two did not prevent him from seeing that totalitarian doctrines share certain characteristics with religious cults and, more directly to the point insofar as we are concerned here, that they require the abolition of the very secularism slowly conquered in the preceding centuries. As Condorcet predicted, this new attack differed both from theocracy and from caesaropapism, inasmuch as the latter conflated the spiritual and the temporal and yet maintained the distinction between the two, requiring only that one yield to the other, whereas the new political religions eliminated the distinction and sacralized either the political power itself, in the form of the state, the people, or the party, or the regime that it imposed, namely, fascism, Nazism or Communism. Traditional religion was fought and eliminated (in Communism) or subjugated and marginalized (in fascism and Nazism). In no case was it allowed to remain the privileged mediator of the sacred, since this role was henceforth reserved to the political power.

If spiritual power, once vanquished, had been able to avoid being eliminated entirely, it could have exercised a restraining force, no matter how modest. None of which was possible in this case because we are dealing here not with subjugation but with a replacement. As Waldemar Gurian notes, 'the energies and forces which formerly had their outlet and expression in religion, limiting the old despotic ruler, are now driving forces behind and in the new despotic regimes of the twentieth century. The totalitarian ideologies replace and supersede religion.'[43] We might add with the benefit of hindsight that Communist regimes go from an initial 'theocratic' stage during which the party controls the state to a second 'caesaro-papist' stage when the party serves the state. In both cases, bearing out Condorcet's fears, this new type of fusion between temporal and spiritual power, precisely because of its totalitarian grip, eliminates more radically than ever before the individual freedom that secularism ensures.

The enemies of secular society are many. In the time of the Enlightenment, they were representatives of the institutional Church who drew inspiration from Bossuet's emblematic declaration, 'I have the right to persecute you because I am right and you are wrong', that established a strong continuity between the spiritual world (where right and wrong could eventually be decided) and the temporal world (where persecutions could be enforced). Tolerance, Bonald argued in the wake of the Revolution, applies only to matters of indifference; when it comes to anything of real importance, we have to submit to the truth of dogma. In totalitarian regimes, secularism is also rejected and society is entirely subjected to the state.

All contemporary Western societies practise various forms of secularism, although it has increasingly come under attack since the nineties with the rise of Islamism.

The spread of a fundamentalist version of the Muslim religion has had two major interrelated consequences on the life of many countries: terrorist acts, which are not specifically aimed against secularism, and the subjugation of women, which is. The latter is not exclusively Islamic, since it can be found all over the world, and more specifically throughout a vast geographical area that includes the Mediterranean and the Middle East and where different religions are practised. Nevertheless, in contemporary Europe, the principle of women's inequality is mainly advocated by certain representatives of Islam. In this case, a literalist interpretation of their sacred texts leads them to justify the domination of men – fathers, brothers or husbands – over adult women and to deprive the latter of individual liberties enjoyed by non-Muslim women, citizens of the same country. The threat denounced by Beccaria becomes a reality here.

This interpretation leads them to idolize virginity and fidelity to the point that young women are deprived of control over their own bodies and married women are prohibited from working outside or even leaving their homes where they may be exposed to the gaze of strangers. Worse still, women are beaten for transgressing these rules, in accordance with religious prescriptions, as certain representatives of fundamentalist Islam have publicly maintained. Witness, for instance, the declarations made by Hani Ramadan, then head of the Islamic Centre in Geneva, who argued that the religious law showed clemency insofar as 'stoning is only in cases of adultery when there are four ocular witnesses to the crime'.[44] How many others think as he does but dare not say so in public?

A number of Muslim women have protested against this situation. In France, the organisation 'Ni putes ni soumises' ('Neither whores nor submissives') has taken up this specific combat. In 2002 it organized a national demonstration and published a manifesto in which its founders declared that they were 'neither whores nor submissives, but simply women who wanted to use their freedom to further their yearning for justice'.[45]

Families not imams subjugate women, but they find justification for their prohibitions in Islamic teachings. The result is that the freedom of these women is restricted and so in the end is equality between the members of society. Among the similar combats in defence of women being fought in countries throughout Europe, one in

particular drew much international attention, Ayaan Hirsi
Ali, a young woman from Somalia, raised as a devout
Muslim, became a member of the Dutch Parliament by
fighting to protect and help women who had been beaten,
raped and mutilated. She raised awareness of the sufferings inflicted upon these women and provoked a useful
debate in society. The country's laws apply to all its citizens, regardless of origin or religion, and all have the
same rights. It is completely intolerable in a liberal
democ-racy to have women oppressed by men and
prevented from acting on their own initiative. Regrettably
Hirsi Ali's activism took a more radical turn that led her
to a wholesale condemnation of the Muslim religion; this
in turn has undermined her impact on devout Muslim
women.

Alongside such rejections of secularism, distortions of
it through oversimplification and abusive systematization
can also be observed. This would be the case if secular
society were to rhyme with a society that banishes
anything that smacks of the sacred. In traditional society,
the sacred was defined by religious dogma and could be
extended to institutions as well as objects. The French
Revolution attempted to sacralize the nation. Love of

one's country was supposed to play the role attributed before to the love of God. Totalitarian regimes tried in turn to sacralize worldly substitutes for the divine, such as the people, the party or the working class. Contemporary liberal democracies do not eliminate all the duties of citizens, but they do not sacralize them either. This does not prevent individuals from finding sacredness in the private sphere: some people consider their work sacred, others vacations, their children, their religion, etc. But no institution and no object is sacred: everything is open to criticism; even subjects that elicit unanimous value judgements in French society, like the genocide of the Jews or the Resistance, do not have a sacred character in the public arena. What is sacred cannot be touched, whereas for the society as a whole there must be no forbidden areas, nothing that impedes the progress of knowledge.

This does not mean, however, that nothing in our secular societies is sacred, simply that it is no longer found in dogmas or in relics but rather in the rights of human beings. A certain form of individual freedom is sacred to us, including the right to practise (or not) a religion of one's own choosing, to criticize institutions and to search for truth in one's own way. Human life is sacred, which is why states have been divested of their right to apply the death penalty. The integrity of the human body is sacred, which is why torture, even for reasons of state, is prohibited, as is excision on young girls who do not yet have their autonomy of will.

Thus, the sacred is not absent from the personal sphere in a secular society or from its legal sphere. And as far as the public sphere is concerned, it is neither dominated by the sacred nor doomed to the chaos of contradictory opinions; it can be regulated by maxims that pertain to general consensus. As Condorcet wrote, 'the real limits of knowledge at every epoch are marked not by the particular reason of some man of genius [...], but by the common reason of enlightened men.'[46] Not all opinions are equally worthy, and one must not confuse eloquent speech with accuracy of thought. Enlightenment can be attained not by relying on one enlightened individual but by bringing together two conditions: firstly, choosing 'enlightened men', that is to say, well-informed individuals capable of reasoning; then, prompting them to look for 'common reason', which means putting them into a situation of developing and exchanging arguments.

In this respect, it may very well be that we still have a long way to go before achieving the ideal of the Enlightenment.

five

Truth

To better define the place of autonomy, it may be opportune to start from a distinction between two types of acts, and hence also of discourses: the aim of one is to promote good; the other aspires to establish truth. Enlightenment thinkers felt the need to draw this distinction in order to remove the knowledge of man and the world from the control of religion. This is why Voltaire draws our attention to the fact that religions are many (he speaks of 'sects') while science is one. Indeed, who has ever heard of algebraist sects? This readily observable difference between two kinds of acts has many implications, and notably it means that the holders of power, be they of divine or human origin, must have no control over discourse aimed at knowing the truth: the two do not belong to the same space. 'Though all human race should for ever conclude, that the sun moves, and the earth remains at rest,' wrote David Hume in 1742, 'the sun stirs not an inch from his place for all these reasonings; and such conclusions are eternally false and erroneous.'[47] Truth cannot be obtained by a vote.

Condorcet explored the consequences of this choice in his thoughts on instruction in the last years of the eighteenth century. He had already tackled the subject before setting out to write his *Mémoires*, when some ten years earlier he penned a defence of religious tolerance and more particularly of the right of Protestants to instruct pupils in the same way as Catholic professors. On what did he base his argument? On the fact that the religion of the teacher is indifferent as long as the subject being taught is a matter of science not faith. 'As much as it is respectable to entrust an ecclesiastic dignity to men of irreproachable orthodoxy, it would be ridiculous to worry about the orthodoxy of a professor of physics and anatomy.'[48] To teach Newton's theories, what does it matter if the professor is Catholic or Protestant? But accepting this principle compels us to the following conclusion: a clear boundary separates two types of subjects that can be taught. On one side are religions, or more generally, opinions and values, all of which are related to individual will or beliefs; on the other, subjects of knowledge whose end purpose is not goodness but truth. Teaching one type or the other corresponds to two distinct activities.

In 1791, while working on his *Mémoires*, Condorcet found two terms for these forms of teaching; he drew a distinction between 'public instruction' and 'national education' and pleaded in favour of the former, the only one in his opinion that fell within the province of Republican competencies. *Education* 'embraces all political, moral, or religious opinions'; *national* education will impart the same patriotic spirit to all pupils. *Instruction* will no longer set out to 'consecrate established opinions' and 'to make men admire unequivocal legislation'; it will teach them 'to subject to free examination' their own convictions, to evaluate and eventually to correct them. Education aims to spread its values and promote what it considers useful. Instruction teaches 'truths of fact and calculation'; it opens the way to objective information and offers the tools that allow people to put their reason to good use so that they can 'decide for themselves'.[49] The goal is individual autonomy, the capacity to examine in a critical way existing norms and choose one's rules of conduct or laws; the means is mastering basic intellectual skills and acquiring knowledge of the world. This is what is involved in the passage from childhood to adulthood. Defending the individual's freedom implies recognizing the difference between fact and interpretation, science and opinion, truth and ideology. It is by calling on the first term in these oppositions, the one that escapes the control of human will and hence of power, that this combat has a chance of succeeding.

Condorcet's reasoning presupposed our fundamental dichotomy between the sphere of the will, which aspires to good, and the sphere of knowledge, which focuses on truth. The former is exemplarily embodied in political acts; the latter in science. The two follow different lines of reasoning, and Condorcet went so far as to maintain that 'generally speaking, power, regardless of its nature, regardless in whose hands it has been confided and regardless of the manner in which it has been conferred, is naturally the enemy of enlightenment'. The reason for this conflict seemed simple to him: the more enlightened people are, the more capable they are of deciding for themselves and the less they will tend to submit blindly to power. 'Truth is at once the enemy of power and of those who exercise it.'[50] Yet not all ruling powers are the same. Good governments are more concerned with the well-being of their subjects than with their own triumph, so they foster the progress of enlightenment and hence of the public instruction that enables their subjects to acquire autonomy by facilitating access to truth. It is indeed a paradoxical government that gives its citizens if not the rod to beat it with then at least the means to emancipate itself. In this respect, it is comparable to parents who strive to make their children autonomous even though they know that by their very success they risk becoming useless as parents and creating distance between them and their offspring.

A wise government does not oppose the growth and spread of knowledge. But that is where its role ends. In no case is it to go so far as to contribute itself to the progress of truth, because truth is not a question of will. The political authority must not teach its choices disguised as truths. 'Its duty is to bring the whole force of truth to bear against error, which is always a public evil; but it does not have the right to decide where truth resides or where error is to be found.'[51] It must make the progress of knowledge materially possible, not establish knowledge itself. It is not up to the people to pronounce what is true or false; it is not up to parliament to deliberate over the meaning of historical facts; it is not up to the government to decide what is to be taught in school. The collective will or the sovereignty of the people comes up against a limit here, which is that of truth, over which it has no leverage. At the same time, the independence of truth protects individual autonomy, since individuals can claim vis-à-vis the ruling power that they have truth on their side. Truth is above laws. Reciprocally, a country's laws do not follow from an established truth: they are the expression of public will, which is always subject to variation. The search for truth is not a matter of public deliberation, and vice versa. Modern states have followed this principle in separating legislative powers, contingent upon popular will alone, and regulatory powers, in which other factors are involved.

The political life in a republic and the autonomy of its

citizens are threatened by two symmetrical opposing dangers: moralism and scientism. Moralism reigns when the good prevails over truth and, under the pressure of the will, facts become malleable materials. Scientism carries the day when values seem to proceed from knowledge and political choices are passed off as scientific deductions. Condorcet warned against the moralist temptation. Alarmed by the enthusiasm of the revolutionaries who pictured contemporary France as a new Sparta, he affirmed the independence of science and of the quest for enlightenment. The Terror, which was a period of extreme moralism when the exigency of virtue left no room for any independent form of truth, eventually triumphed over Condorcet's resistance, for he perished in its reign. But he himself did not always avoid the scientist illusion, for he hoped that the progress of knowledge alone would generate the best political order and the happiness of mankind.

Scientism is a philosophical and political doctrine born with modernity that works on the assumption that the world is completely knowable, and hence also that it can be transformed to meet the objectives that we set for ourselves, which are themselves deduced from our knowledge of the world. In a sense it assumes that the good derives from truth. The scientistic temptation was already present at the time of the Enlightenment. It was manifested, for instance, in Diderot's moral philosophy, which set up the laws of 'nature' as the only laws that we should have to obey. 'Civil law ought only to be the enunciation of the laws of nature. [...] what makes man as he is [...] ought to be the basis of the morality suitable for him.'[52] And what can help us know nature better than science? What should be is automatically deduced from what is. Some years later, Sade used this reasoning to legitimate his own distortion of the spirit of the Enlightenment. 'Destruction being one of the chief laws of nature, nothing that destroys can be criminal.' 'For a bridle have nothing but your inclinations, for laws only your desires, for morality Nature's alone.'[53] Diderot and Sade reasoned as if a human being lived alone, as if her acts had no effect on other human beings; they could consequently regard all civil or moral laws as superfluous.

The same reasoning was applied to the political arena. For Holbach, human beings are unhappy because they do not know nature. From this, we may conclude that such knowledge is necessary and sufficient to make people happy, that knowledge is all it takes to live well. For his part, Condorcet maintained that, 'knowing the truth in order to make the order of society conform to it, this is the sole source of public happiness'.[54] Acutely aware of the hold of the good over truth, Condorcet had no objection to making truth 'the sole source' of the good; public action in the social arena had no need to call on particular values or objectives, he thought, since it would follow entirely from the knowledge of truth.

Other Enlightenment thinkers opposed the scientism that was just beginning to emerge during the age of Enlightenment. We have already seen that Montesquieu considered vain any attempt to master the world fully, due to the world's extreme complexity and also to the singular nature of one of its inhabitants, the human being. Humans are never entirely predictable because they are ever ready to elude determinisms; they are always capable of 'acquiescing or resisting', to borrow Rousseau's terms. Dispelling the illusion of an automatic continuity between accumulated knowledge and moral and political perfection was even the starting point of Rousseau's thinking, and in this respect he opposed a good number of his contemporaries, encyclopaedists and 'philosophers'. Rousseau relentlessly repeated that to improve humanity, 'spreading enlightenment' was not enough. 'We can be men without being scholars.'[55]

Certain forms of scientism, which were seriously challenged by twentieth-century totalitarianism, are now rejected by all: no one advocates the elimination of inferior races or of reactionary classes. This does not mean that contemporary democracies are free from all traces of scientism, simply that it assumes other forms. One of these is the temptation to rely on 'experts' to formulate moral norms or political objectives, as if the definition of what is good proceeds from knowledge. This is also true of the 'sociobiological' project to absorb the knowledge of human beings into the knowledge of nature and to ground moral and political conduct in the laws of physics and biology. There is reason to wonder why biologists are deemed so qualified to sit on the different ethics committees that have been established in Western countries. These boards are usually made up of two categories of specialists, scientists and religious authorities, as if no political body and no moral authority existed between the two.

Such choices evidence a monolithic conception of

social space, according to which it would suffice to have the right information to make the right decisions. But in point of fact, information itself is far from homogeneous and no purely quantitative approach is satisfying. Having ever greater amounts of information at our fingertips not only does not make us more virtuous, as Rousseau already predicted, but it does not even make us more knowledgeable. The staggering increase in data storage and transmission has revealed a new danger: too much information kills information. All you have to do is ask a question on the Internet and you immediately have hundreds and thousands of replies. How do you know which is most trustworthy and enlightening? Is an encyclopaedia freely written by its users (Wikipedia) preferable to one written by competent scientists? Only if you erase the boundary between *vouloir* and *savoir*, between desire and knowledge.

Moreover, there are other paths to knowledge than science. To gain insight into the mysterious workings of human behaviour, a great novel can be more enlightening than a sociological study. Some Enlightenment thinkers understood this. Vico, for example, asserted that knowledge in certain subjects could be more readily acquired through myth and poetry than through abstract thinking. This heterogeneity in the paths to knowledge, in the quality of information and in the forms of social intervention also compromises the ambitions of scientism.

Moralism, which involves in this case the subjugation of the search for truth to the needs of the good, is much older than the Enlightenment and is directly opposed to its spirit. And yet it has clearly survived it. This can be illustrated by the debate in France about the writing of twentieth-century history that has resurfaced periodically in the recent past. In 2005 a group of deputies introduced a bill concerning the interpretation given to the French colonial enterprise and in particular the occupation of Algeria. One of the articles stipulated, 'school programmes [must] recognize the positive role of the French presence abroad, especially in North Africa'. The bill was passed on 23 February 2005 and was reconfirmed by a majority of deputies on 29 November of the same year. In this way, a reading of the past was submitted to a vote and acquired force of law, which meant that anyone who opposed it could be brought to court. Like the Church in the seventeenth century prohibiting Galileo from the free pursuit of truth, here

were French deputies in the twenty-first century pre-
scribing the content of historical study to historians and
to the students and professors who benefited from their
research. Hume's warnings were clearly forgotten: truth
here was being designated by a vote.

It was shocking to see that this bill mentioned only the
'positive role' of colonization, euphemistically called 'the
French presence abroad'. Anyone who steps outside the
ethnocentric nationalist perspective would be hard put to
find a positive side to invading a foreign country under
false pretences, keeping its population in a state of legal
inferiority, in disregard for the very Republican principles
that were advocated in Metropolitan France, and repress-
ing attempts to achieve independence through massacres
and torture – all of which are well-established facts and
had been for a long time. What was perhaps even more
regrettable was to see that, half a century after the end of
the colonies, the complexity of history was being reduced
to such adjectives of pure moral judgement as 'positive'
and 'negative', thereby imposing an optimistic or
pessimistic world-view. Such a Manichean simplification
inevitably betrays the experience of millions of people
for more than a century. The study of history can never

totally ignore the values that permeate human existence, but it cannot be reduced to such clear-cut labels. If historians are going to further their understanding, to collect as many facts as possible and formulate the most accurate interpretations, then they must not decide ahead of time what morality they want to see in the end. History comprises very few pages written in black and white only.

What is particularly unsettling to anyone who cherishes the spirit of the Enlightenment is, of course, that parliament undertook to vote on an interpretation of history as if all it took was a political majority to determine the truth of a proposition. And this vote ended up making the assertion more vulnerable (since another majority could reject it). In the presence of science, sects disappear, Voltaire said; in the presence of truth, parties have nothing to say, because representatives of the people are not in the best position to seek truth. Truth is not a matter of will. What makes an elected representative competent to judge history? Is it parliament's role to decide on the right reading of past events or facts? That these questions need even to be asked shows how outrageously anachronistic the vote on this bill was.

The fact is that the French deputies were not at their

first try. A few years earlier they had decided that Turkey was guilty of the Armenian genocide and that slavery was a crime against humanity. And a few years before that they voted in a bill, which was probably the first of its kind, making the negation of the genocide of the Jews during World War II a punishable offence. The events in question may lend themselves to less controversy than the colonization of the Maghreb, but the question of principle is the same. State power has no right to decide where truth lies, Condorcet maintained. The French parliament seems to have forgotten this elementary principle. To take a proposition out of the field of investigation of truth, to include it in a catechism and attach penal sanctions to it, is to degrade it, not to strengthen it.

Truth cannot dictate the good but neither should it be subjugated to it. Scientism and moralism are both alien to the spirit of the Enlightenment. But a third danger exists, and that is that the very notion of truth be considered irrelevant. In a study on 1984, the philosopher Leszek Kolakowski praised Orwell for having recognized the importance of the challenge to truth in totalitarian regimes. It is not only that political leaders in such regimes occasionally resorted to lies – this they did everywhere. It is that the very distinction between truth and falsehood, between truth and fiction, became superfluous in light of the purely pragmatic considerations of usefulness and convenience. This is why in such regimes science was no longer immune to ideological attacks and the notion of objective information had lost its meaning. Not only was history rewritten as a function of the needs of the moment, but also biological and physical discoveries were denied if they were deemed inappropriate. It 'is the great cognitive triumph of totalitarianism. By managing to abrogate the very idea of truth, it can no longer be accused of lying,' Kolakowski concluded.[56] This time the ruling authorities had definitively disposed of the impertinent truth.

One might think that this presents a danger in totalitarian countries, not in democracies. But several recent episodes in the United States illustrate the new fragility of truth.

The first event of this nature was the decision in certain schools to teach the theory of evolution based on Darwin's work and the biblical myth of creation (or 'intelligent design' as it is called) as two 'hypotheses' equally worthy of respect. In a country where, according to polls, 73 per cent of the population believe in life after death and 39 per cent think that the Bible was directly dictated by God and should be taken literally,[57] it is not surprising that many people prefer the biblical version to the biological one. But the convictions of the individual concern that individual alone and have validity only in the private arena: this is, moreover, in keeping with the spirit and the letter of the American constitution. On the other hand, a decision about the education programme in a given school concerns the local community, and the latter refused to see the qualitative difference between scientific discourse and fiction, between *logos* and *muthos*. And yet they remained cautious and did not take their reasoning to its logical extreme: they did not have anything to say about the medical care given in hospitals, for instance, even though it is based on the same biological sciences that creationist theory challenges.

A second example of the change in the status of truth, seemingly unrelated to the first, was provided by a recent political event: the justification of the war against Iraq based on the weapons of mass destruction that it was said to have. We know now that no such weapons existed, but that is not the crux of the problem since their presence was possible. Several things remain troubling about this episode. We have learned since that government officials did everything they could to convince Americans that these weapons existed, exhibiting as proof evidence they knew to be flimsy and trying to compromise individuals who brought information that contradicted their claims. In other words, people in the government knew that what they were saying was not true, but they said it anyway, no doubt because they thought that doing so would be useful to their country. This contempt for the truth was confirmed by Paul Wolfowitz, one of the people involved, when he admitted that the weapons of mass destruction argument was chosen because it was the one that could most easily galvanize support from a large majority of the population. He did not even mention the question of the truth of the argument. Just as totalitarian ideologists considered truth irrelevant, so did Wolfowitz.

The kind of ordinary official lie that politicians tell when they claim that they are not cheating on their wives is a disguised homage to truth, because every effort is made to simulate truth. The case in point, on the other hand, exemplifies indifference to veracity. And it is all the more disturbing because it is not an isolated case.

There were other pretensions that testified to this change in the status of truth, like the claim that the spirit of international conventions on war prisoners was being respected in the Guantanamo detention camp or that every day Iraq was taking great strides towards peace and democracy. In another area altogether, we learned some time ago that the federal government deliberately altered information on a number of scientific reports on global warming that did not substantiate its position on the Kyoto protocol. The fact is that when the status of truth is manipulated, we cannot be said to be living in a liberal democracy any more. How are we to understand such an attack on the foundations of democracy? A number of these assertions disconnected from any relationship to truth became acceptable because they were made in a situation of crisis that required a national consensus, and hence the suspension of critical judgement on the part of those whose profession it was to provide trustworthy information, namely journalists. This crisis has been going on since 11 September 2001. An upsurge in the spirit of patriotism and a rise in the fear of 'phantoms', to para-phrase Condorcet, sufficed to thrust aside the very concern for truth that is constitutive of the democratic space.

Of course, the United States government is not the only one to prefer victory to truth; nonetheless it is legitimate to choose this example over others, since the United States stands as the single greatest military and political power of our time. And great power engenders great dangers, since it gives those who have it the feeling that they are always right and need not take into account the opinion of others. To avoid the abyss into which the lure of power risks drawing it and, with it, the rest of the world, even the most powerful country has to recognize that truth is not something to tamper with.

six

Humanity

AUTONOMY ALONE CANNOT SUFFICE TO CHARAC-
terize the Enlightenment's ideal conception of human
conduct. Clearly, it was considered better to be guided by
one's own will than by a rule that came from elsewhere, but
to go where? All desires and all acts are not equally worthy.
And since people could no longer turn to heaven to find
out what was right and what was wrong, they would have
to stick to worldly realities. The shift was from a distant end
– God – to a closer one, which, Enlightenment philosophy
proclaimed, was humanity itself. Whatever contributes to
the welfare of human beings was deemed good.

Such an assertion represents not so much a rejection of the Christian doctrine as a revision thereof. Christianity posited the equivalence of two loves, the love of God and the love of one's neighbour. St Paul proclaimed many times that 'one who loves another has fulfilled the law'. All that Enlightenment thinkers did was to affirm that for them one of the terms of this equation was good enough. 'It's enough to hold to Christian love,' Lessing declared in 1777, 'what happens to the Christian religion does not matter.' The doctrinal and institutional framework was what was rejected, not the content that it brought to the fore. It was the same deist spirit that Benjamin Franklin illustrated ten years later when he maintained that 'the most acceptable service to God is doing good to man'. Love of human beings no longer required divine justification. When told that his offer of hospitality, if made for Christ's sake, would be rewarded, Franklin replied, 'Don't let me be mistaken. It was not for *Christ*'s sake but for *your sake*.'[58]

Human beings became the horizon of human activity, the focal point towards which everything converged. When Diderot asked himself about the underlying principle of his encyclopaedic project, he saw only one, and that was man. This was already the case of the universe that the *Encyclopédie* strove to comprehend and represent. 'Why should we not introduce man as he is placed in the universe?' Diderot asks. 'Why should we not make him the common centre?'[59] It was at once a right and a duty: man was to be the centre of the work because he is the centre of the world, or rather, because it is man who constructs its meaning. Consequently, his existence ceased to be a mere means in the service of a higher purpose, be it the salvation of his soul or the coming of the city of God; the purpose of human beings was to be found within. 'Man,' Rousseau had his heroine Julie say, 'is too noble a being to have to serve merely as an instrument of others.'[60] This new place for man, now pitted as an absolute against *things* that are only relative, led Kant to his famous principle of humanist morality: 'the human being and in general every rational being exists as an end in itself, not merely as a means to be used by this or that will at its discretion; instead he must in all his actions, whether directed to himself or also to other rational beings, always be regarded at the same time as an end.'[61]

The word that designates human well-being on this earth is happiness. With the Enlightenment its pursuit became legitimate, replacing the search for salvation. 'Oh happiness! Our being's end and aim!' exclaimed Alexander Pope in his *Essay on Man*.[62] It is striking to see how, despite the diversity of literary genres, countries of origin and convictions of their authors, the European texts written in this period present a natural world in which human beings have to face purely human hostile forces and strive to find fulfilment in their worldly existence. The best citizen is the one who 'contributes to the happiness of the world', Voltaire declared.[63] Philosophical treatises, novels, poems and plays evinced the difficulties of a purely human world. Paintings depicted the charms of rural life, private delights, the joys of villagers, domestic bliss: in sum, human pleasures.

Where is one to look for the keys to happiness? The majority of philosophers and writers were not content to promote social reforms; they also gave pride of place to individual experiences, and among these, to affections insofar as they create bonds between the individual and others. 'Destroy love and friendship, what remains in the world worth accepting?' asks Hume.[64] A beautiful life is a life full of love. And this is not a matter of quantity: Hume pictured King Solomon a deeply unhappy man surrounded by 700 wives and 300 concubines. One wife or one mistress and a few well-chosen friends would have enabled him to experience the fullness of his humanity. 'I don't believe that someone who does not love can be happy,' Rousseau agrees. Happiness is therefore accessible to everyone. All it takes is loving and being loved. And consequently it is fragile. We need the affection of others to live but nothing can guarantee its permanence. The more filled with affection a person's life is, the more vulnerable he or she is. 'The more attachments he has, the greater his sorrow.'[65] Such is the nature of human happiness, and there's nothing one can do to guarantee it.

In the late eighteenth century, an attempt was made to set up happiness as the goal not only of the individual's life but also of the government and of the state. The 'pursuit of happiness' was to figure in the American Declaration of Independence. In a memoir written in France in 1787, Lavoisier, a remarkable chemist and prominent politician, proclaimed that 'the true end of a government should be to increase the joy, happiness and well-being of all individuals'. Two years later, he declared in a speech to the Estates-General, 'The object of every social institution is to make all those who live under its laws as happy as possible. Happiness must not be reserved to a small number of people. It belongs to all.'[66] The Revolution, to which Lavoisier was to fall victim, would show that it was not advisable to put all of human existence into the care of the government. The principle nonetheless holds true that the social institutions of a country must serve the men and women who live there.

Since then, the situation has changed again. The twentieth-century totalitarian regimes abundantly demonstrated the danger of entrusting the state with responsibility for individual happiness. But the ultimate victory of democratic states has had a surprising consequence. Insofar as this political system does not claim to embody sovereign good, people have stopped pinning their hopes of worldly happiness and self-fulfilment on political structures at all. It is precisely because democracy won that it no longer arouses passion. Individual autonomy came out of these trials reinforced and all people ask of the state is simply to eliminate obstacles to individual happiness, not to ensure it. No longer a harbinger of hope, the state has become a mere service provider. People may well lack a common religious framework or belief in a revolution that could bring happiness to all, but they have not given up on their desire to make their lives more beautiful and rich in meaning. It is just that the paths they take are those they have individually chosen.

This reversal of perspective as to the end purpose of our acts, this shift from the divine to the human, can only be compared in its radicality to the Copernican revolution that put the Sun in the place of the Earth, except that in our case the human being was moved closer to the centre rather than away from it. Not surprisingly this reversal elicited strong opposition from those who defended the existing hierarchy, from Bonald to John Paul II. They feared that, without the central reference to God, there would be a breakdown of society. If God is dead, everything is permissible. For order to prevail, God's rights must supplant human rights. The totalitarian ideology, in its turn, rejected Enlightenment humanism: the goal of the society was not so much 'the happiness of all individuals' as an abstraction: a regenerated people, the Communist state and a glorious future.

The distortions of the humanist spirit of the Enlightenment assumed an even greater variety of forms. They were also already present in the eighteenth century. Once again, it was Sade who voiced the most extreme formulations. Starting from the premise that man is a legitimate end to human activity, Sade engaged in a twofold reduction: first, he reduced happiness to sexual pleasure; second, he reduced humanity to the isolated individual, the desiring subject. 'No limits to your pleasure save those of your strength and will.'[67] Nothing then was to limit individual autonomy, which aspires solely to the intensity of experience as it is happening; the world was thereby reduced to the here and now. In a less hyperbolic form, this reasoning was shared by many libertines of the period. Rousseau, on the other hand, frontally opposed this outlook, firstly because he could not imagine a society that could do without a regulatory system to control the forces and wills of its members. 'Tell me then at what crime will a man stop who has no law but his heart's desires, who knows not how to resist his heart's passions?' Moreover, Rousseau was perfectly aware that individual self-sufficiency is an illusion. 'Each will feel that his happiness is not inside him, that it depends on all that surrounds him.'[68] The problem with sensualist and egocentrist doctrines is not so much that they are immoral as that they are mistaken. Admittedly, Western societies often seem to resemble the caricatures that their religious opponents in the West and the East have of them; in particular, they seem to be exclusively preoccupied with material success, with money and with the pleasures that money can buy. But to deplore this attitude, there is no need to bring up God. It suffices to recall that human needs are actually manifold and varied.

Here the spirit of the Enlightenment consisted in reducing the distance between action and its end purpose. The latter was brought from heaven down to earth to be embodied in humanity not in God, alongside acts that were themselves human and earthbound. Distortions of this spirit involved eliminating not only the divine purpose but all sense of purpose to focus solely on movement for movement's sake, strength for the sake of strength, and will for the sake of will. Our time has become, in many respects, one of forgetting ends and sacralizing means. Perhaps the clearest example of this is provided by the development of science. It is not because a piece of scientific work serves directly or indirectly specifically human goals, such as happiness, emancipation or peace, that it will be promoted and financed; it is because it demonstrates the scientist's virtuosity. It seems as if the mere fact that something is possible means that it has to become a reality. Why go to Mars otherwise? The economy works on the same principle of development for development's sake and growth for growth's sake. Can political authorities content themselves with accepting this strategy? For a number of decades already, it has been yielding questionable results in Third World countries and its repercussions are being felt in Western industrialized countries too. Must we accept the triumph of finance capitalism, with its consequences: globalization and delocalizations? Are these in our best interests or are we caught up in a movement that has run away with itself?

A similar loss of purpose sometimes seems to affect politics in liberal democracies and one wonders if people who pursue political careers seek power to serve ideals or for themselves, their sole goal being to keep it as long as possible? Of course, this dilemma is not new, but it has become an even more burning issue today. A case in point was provided by the 2005 French referendum on the European constitution. The positions adopted by both sides, the 'yes' and the 'no', were not self-evident. There was even reason to wonder at the French president Jacques Chirac's decision to hold such a referendum. He knew that his party had lost the two preceding elections and that there was a risk of defeat in this case too. He also knew that a parliamentary vote, a fully acceptable way of getting approval for the text, would have been in his favour; since all of the parties represented in parliament were in favour of the constitution project, it would have been voted in by about 90 per cent of the representatives. So why then did the French president deliberately choose to risk defeat? There is every reason to believe that he made a purely tactical decision: submitting the question to a referendum enabled him to divide the opposition and hence to weaken it, in advance of the 2007 presidential election. And so he sacrificed the European constitution, which he probably sincerely advocated, to personal ambition, to his desire to keep power in his hands or in the hands of his supporters.

On the other side, Laurent Fabius, a prominent member of the opposition, took a similar course of action. A member of the Socialist party who had fallen out with its leadership, Fabius was the only important political figure to take a stand against the European constitution. Known until then for his pro-European positions, his campaign to vote no created some surprise, and gave people the impression that he too could not take his sights off the 2007 presidential elections. Apparently, his primary goal was to impose himself as the incontrovertible candidate of all of the Left. For this purpose, he had to cast a wide net, especially in the direction of all those who stood to the left of the Socialist party. Although he was probably attached to the construction of Europe, he opted to advocate what was called the *non de gauche*, or the no on the left vote. Both Chirac and Fabius acted in view of acquiring power instead of putting this power in the service of a higher ideal.

The movement that consists in progressively bringing a goal closer to what should be the means of attaining it, or, to put it differently, of turning the means into the goal, was already beginning to emerge in the eighteenth century, but it was then oddly confined to one particular area, that of art, and especially of painting. Indeed, the thinking that is contained in art's mode of representing the world always seems to precede discursive thought by a century or more. The interest in analysing the individual because of his or her uniqueness, independently of the person's attributes, was asserted in the sixteenth century by Montaigne and his contemporaries, when it was already evidenced in painting by the mid-fifteenth century, first in Flemish and then in Italian portraits and self-portraits. Official seventeenth-century discourse in Protestant countries praised domestic virtues as a means to act in accordance with divine commandments, when, at the same time, Dutch painters were depicting a sublimation of the human without any reference to a superior reality, magnifying the gesture of a mother bent over her sick child with concern in her eyes.

In the eighteenth century, the way painting was interpreted changed in nature. People found in it a hymn not to God or even to man, but to art. To the English painter Joshua Reynolds, Michelangelo's paintings on the ceiling of the Sistine Chapel, the product of a mind totally imbued with religious thinking, conveyed 'an idea of the dignity of art'; from that point on, the aim of art became to materialize beauty not virtue. Looking at the same paintings, Goethe had eyes only for the artistic performance and left the doctrinal message aside: 'without having seen the Sistine Chapel one can form no appreciable idea of what one man is capable of achieving'.[69] Painters themselves produced works whose justification seemed to be firstly to grasp the hidden identity of what they were showing, in other words, to produce beauty. Witness Watteau's dreamers, Chardin's still lifes, Gainsborough's landscapes and Fragonard's imaginary portraits.

In so doing, both painters and beholders of their paintings contented themselves with highlighting a dimension of painting that had always been present but that had been ignored in earlier centuries, namely the art of painting itself. This discovery led at times to what is called 'art for art's sake'. But politics and the economy must not obey the same imperatives as art: we can admire a politician's style or an entrepreneur's capabilities; we must nevertheless judge them on the results of their acts. When art is aware of the laws inherent to it, it does not stand in opposition to the spirit of the Enlightenment. On the other hand, when science or politics leaves aside the human finalities of its action, it endangers this spirit and the good that we expect from it.

seven

Universality

Freedom of action is restricted by its necessarily human finality but also by the awareness of the fact that all human beings belong to the same species and that consequently they have the same right to dignity. This imperative takes on a different meaning if we think of it in terms of the citizens of a country or the inhabitants of planet earth.

When Rousseau looked at the society around him, he saw neither equality of rights nor equality in actual fact. This is what motivated him to write his first general reflection on the human condition, *Discourse on the*

Origin and Foundations of Inequality Among Men, which concludes with the following harsh observation: 'It is manifestly against the Law of Nature [...] that a handful of people abound in superfluities while the starving multitude lacks in necessities.' Merely to imagine the beginnings of a redistribution of wealth, one has to situate oneself in the framework of a just state, which wasn't the case for the country where Rousseau lived. Rousseau set out to think about the manner in which such a state should be organized and ended in *The Social Contract* with the imperative of strict equality before the law. 'The social contract establishes amongst citizens such an equality, that they are all engaged under the same conditions, and must all enjoy the same rights.'[70] The will that governs the country cannot be general unless no voice is excluded.

Mid-eighteenth-century France was far from meeting this criterion. Its population was divided into castes that did not enjoy the same privileges: women did not have the same rights as men, and slaves had none at all. The principle that Rousseau set forth took time to be put into effect. The idea of equality between citizens was established in part in 1789 and more completely in 1848, the year slavery was abolished. Women weren't given the right to vote until 1944. This equality before the law did not suffice to eliminate all forms of discrimination and the demand for equality is still of present-day relevance. Our struggles in this direction still draw inspiration from the Enlightenment project and pursue those initiated two or three centuries ago. Daniel Defoe already maintained that the inferiority of women was due solely to the fact that they were barred from education. Helvetius was also persuaded that women were men's equals by nature. Condorcet argued that boys and girls should be given the same courses in the same places by the same professors, whether they were men or women, and he held that women should not be barred from any career.

Enlightenment thinkers condemned slavery even if they did not initiate an effective fight against it. 'Nor is slavery less opposed to the civil law than to that of nature,' Montesquieu declared. Rousseau brushed aside all of the usual justifications given to support this practice. 'The terms *slavery* and *right* contradict and exclude each other.' Condorcet begins his *Reflections on Negro Slavery* (written using the pseudonym Monsieur Schwartz) with the words, 'To reduce a man to slavery, to purchase him, to sell him, to keep him in servitude, these are veritable crimes, and they are crimes worse than theft.'[71] At the time of the Revolution, Olympe de Gouges engaged in a twofold struggle for the abolition of slavery and equality of rights for women; she wrote the play *Negro Slavery* and the Declaration of the Rights of Woman and the Female Citizen. She herself earned the right to the guillotine.

Beyond the boundaries of a country, universality took on a different sense. All of the people who live in a country should be its citizens; all of the people living on the earth are human beings from the outset. What they have in common is more essential than what differentiates them. 'I am necessarily a man and I am French by chance,' declared Montesquieu. Those who felt imbued with the spirit of the Enlightenment cherished their belonging to the human species more than their affiliation to their country. Denis Diderot wrote to David Hume on 22 February 1768, 'My dear David, you belong to all nations and you will never ask an unhappy man for his birth certificate. I flatter myself that I am, like you, a citizen of the great city of the world.'[72]

Universality was not only responsible for the image that one could have of oneself. In a world where good and evil could no longer be based on the word of God or on lessons of tradition, it provided a possible legitimation. The allegiance of humanity validated the choice of the good. 'What do you call just and unjust?' Voltaire asked in his *Philosophical Dialogues*, and his answer was, 'That which so appears to the entire universe.' Rousseau interpreted the just and the unjust as effects of altruism and egotism. 'The less the object of our care is directly dependent on ourselves, the less we have to fear from the illusion of self-interest; the more general this interest becomes, the juster it is; and the love of the human race is nothing but the love of justice within us.'[73] Generalization produced the criterion of justice; and it was in this spirit that Kant was to formulate his categorical imperative: an action is good only if it corresponds to a maxim that can be universalized.

Equality is therefore at the basis of the rights of citizens and of the morality of human beings. Do human beings have, in addition, rights that proceed from their mere quality of human beings? This is what certain authors professed, in line with the modern school of natural law that sought the origin of these rights not in a cosmic order or in God's word but in the very fact that we all belong to the same species and are endowed with the same dignity. Christian Wolff, one of the most influential of these authors, maintained in the eighteenth century that a universal right existed, that it is the right 'that belongs to the individual as an individual'.[74] Obviously, these natural rights did not have the same status as the rights that citizens enjoy, because in the absence of a state equipped with a legal apparatus there is nothing to guarantee them. From this standpoint, universal rights are similar to moral principles: they are seen as desirable but are not enforceable. Nonetheless, nothing prevents a state from including human rights in common law or integrating them into its constitution. In this case, they benefit from universal recognition and also acquire force of law inside the country. This was done in the Declaration of Rights of the American states in 1776 and the Declaration of the Rights of Man and the Citizen in France in 1789.

Today, human rights enjoy a great deal of prestige, and nearly all countries like to see themselves as their defenders. This does not prevent even the most eloquent advocates of these rights from rejecting them in practice when circumstances seem to warrant it.

This has been the case for the death penalty. Beccaria

in his *Essay on Crimes and Punishments* most clearly expressed Enlightenment thinking on this subject. Every human being, as a member of the species and not because he or she is the citizen of such and such a country, has a right to life and this right is inalienable. I may have given up my natural freedom to benefit from civil freedom (and protection), but I have never given the community, explicitly or tacitly, the right of life and death over me. What could justify this total suppression of individual will by the collective will? It cannot be the need to prevent the criminal from inflicting harm, since the person must have been arrested and imprisoned already if there is a question of killing him or her. Is it to pay for the crime? This punishment would make sense only if one believes in a form of life after death: in the beyond, the executed person could measure the seriousness of the offence by the severity of the punishment. Such a lesson is necessarily lost on individuals who do not think in these terms.

Another justification that is frequently proposed is the dissuasive value of the supreme punishment for those who are left behind; this is a conception of punishment as an example. Yet no study has confirmed the consistency of this effect and the only Western country that still practises the death penalty, the United States, has the highest rate of criminality. Beccaria doubted that such an effect was possible because, far from opposing the killing that it is supposed to punish, the death penalty imitates it, 'for the hand of the legislator and the assassin were directed by the same spirit of ferocity'. He even argued that this punishment is harmful by the example of cruelty that it gives and the risk of imitation. It is true that in times of war, governments authorize and even encourage their nationals to kill as many enemies as possible. But wars are declared precisely because no negotiated resolution could be found. The rest of the time, citizens of a country live according to the law; to legally imitate military acts is to compromise the very idea of law. 'Is it not absurd, that the laws, which detest and punish homicide, should, in order to prevent murder, publicly commit murder themselves?'[75]

Another transgression of human rights, occasionally practised by governments, is torture. All human beings have the right to the integrity of their bodies. Only they can give up this right by self-mutilation or suicide. Consequently, torture cannot be legalized any more than homicide. Governments that practise it, not by sadism, but to obtain information that they deem indispensable, expect, Beccaria writes, 'that pain should be the test of truth'.[76] The price paid is extremely high since to extract a confession whose value is questionable (people will confess to anything to stop pain), intolerable pain is inflicted on the tortured person who will be marked for life; at the same time the torturer is destroyed internally and loses a sense of universal human community; and, finally, a message is sent to the entire population that the bounds set by law can be transgressed.

The French army systematically practised torture during the Algerian War, in particular after 1957, when it was entrusted with police functions. Its justification was that in a civil war of that kind, the enemies were invisible and extracting information was needed to identify them. Often the 'bomb-about-to-explode-in-the-next-hour' argument was added for further justification, when in fact such cases were exceptional and thousands of people were concerned by the torture that continued long after the presumed attack. Germaine Tillion, the French resister and deportee, but also an anthropologist and historian, who did her best to put a stop to such practices, wrote a letter about torture to the cardinal in Paris in

1957: 'In the last six months, many young Muslim and Christian girls have been tortured for no good reason or for no reason at all: stripped, subjected to bathtub torture, electric torture, sometimes with electrodes placed on the genitals, hands tied behind their back and hung by their wrists, which, like the cross, provokes suffocation.'[77]

This was how the Iraqi prisoner Manadel al-Jamadi died in November 2003, tortured to death in the Abu Ghraib prison in Baghdad by CIA agents. After having six ribs broken and his head wrapped in a plastic bag, he was hung from his wrists, which had been handcuffed behind his back. He suffocated to death less than an hour after he was admitted to prison. Some people have survived to testify about such hangings. This was the case for Jean Améry, imprisoned in Belgium by the Gestapo during World War II, who left a detailed report of his experience in *At the Mind's Limits*. Other prisoners who were released from the Guantanamo camp told how they were beaten, stripped and put in cages, forced to swallow medicine and watch pornographic movies, and intimidated by dogs on leashes held close to the detainees (in a distant echo of the rats brushing against the faces of prisoners in *1984*).

The American secret services are probably not the only

ones to subject their prisoners to torture, but the United States government took an exceptional position when they tried to legalize it. After 9/11, Vice-President Cheney promised to use every means available to combat terrorism. A memo from the justice department of 1 August 2002 listed some of these means: suffocation without causing death, waterboarding, depriving detainees of medicine for wounds, preventing sleep, deafening and blinding. Most of the techniques are mental not physical torture, but they are traumatic: they bring prisoners to the verge of madness and leave indelible traces. Until 2009, the American government systematically refused to treat these terrorists in compliance with the Geneva Convention on prisoners of war. Other documents from the White House made it possible to get around injunctions issued by Congress and the Senate and to continue to practise torture with impunity. And this was done years after the terrorist attacks and the military interventions. What is particularly shocking here is that not only was torture tolerated, but it was advocated as part of the fight for internal security and for human rights, when these were precisely the rights that were being trampled in the process.

The death penalty and torture represent rejections of the universality underpinning the Enlightenment. The distortions of Enlightenment universality manifest a disruption in the balance between universal and particular, between unification and tolerance. The Enlightenment calls for both, and we can assume that this implies that the boundary between the two cannot be set once and for all. If any means will do to impose unity, then the freedom of individuals is threatened.

In past centuries, Enlightenment thought served as a source of inspiration to a liberal, reformist current that stood against conservatism in the name of universality and equal respect for all. Things have changed and now we find conservatives defending a superior Western culture who claim the Enlightenment as their source of inspiration. They see themselves as engaged in a fight against 'relativism', which they believe derives from the Romantic reaction in the early nineteenth century. But, as we can see, they can claim Enlightenment roots only by amputating the real Enlightenment tradition in which universality of values and plurality of cultures are interconnected. It is time to leave clichés behind: Enlightenment thought is not to be conflated with dogmatism (my culture has to be imposed on all) or with nihilism (all cultures are the same). Using this tradition to denigrate others and legitimate subjecting or destroying them is a radical distortion of the Enlightenment.

If human rights are the sole unquestionable reference point in the public arena and the unique yardstick by which the orthodoxy of discourses and acts is judged, then we find ourselves in an arena of political correctness and media lynching, the democratic version of a witch-hunt – a sort of one-upmanship of virtue, the effect of which is to eliminate the expression of thoughts that diverge from it. This moral blackmail lurking in the background of all debates is harmful to democratic life. It leads to the excessive domination of the good over truth, giving, as a result, an appearance of a lie to everything that clamours in the name of good, and an appearance of truth to anything that opposes dominant thinking. And so we find prospering theories of the far right that pride themselves on being the only ones to dare to 'talk straight', simply because they are saying the opposite of what is politically correct. And this is how what can be called the 'politically abject' gains acceptance.

Rights must not be confused with morality, neither

should those who make statements that displease us be dragged into court, as if, as Beccaria put it, 'judges were to be the knights-errant of human nature in general, rather than guardians of particular conventions between men'.[78] For the same reason, international justice must not aspire to the role of universal morality. It must be based on existing agreements and contracts, like those binding the members of the European Union. A right that does not guarantee an enforcement to which the contractual parties have agreed compromises the very idea of a right.

This means that a country is not justified to use violence to restore the law or human rights in a neighbouring country, what is today called 'the right of intervention'. The use of the term 'right' in this expression is peculiar. What would be the source of this right that I give myself to settle other people's affairs if they never granted me such a right? If we are indeed bound by a form of solidarity to all the world's inhabitants, then we have the duty to help, if need be, but not the 'right' to invade the country where people are suffering. The problem here is that the means used defeat the purpose, as in the case of torture practised by the CIA. To avoid such eventualities we have to draw a clear line between proposing and imposing, influencing and forcing, peace and war; the first term does not negate our compassion for the suffering of others; the second does.

One of the immediate precursors of the Enlighten- ment, Pierre Bayle, a French Protestant who was forced to flee Catholic persecution, found the appropriate words to warn all those tempted to employ force to impose good. The good had been defined by the Catholics who, in an attempt to save the souls of Protestants and hence to make them happier, did not hesitate to have recourse to force: this good was so great that it could withstand a few sacrifices (when they concerned others). Bayle had this to say about the injunction from the Gospels, 'compel them to enter' (Luke 14:23) used to justify the persecutions: 'Beat, whip, imprison, and kill the obstinate, and take away their women and children. These appalling crimes in other circumstances, are deemed good when they serve my cause.'[79] A noble end cannot be achieved by ignoble means because the end will be lost on the way. This is what the colonizers were doing when they subjugated entire populations under the pretext of bringing them equality. This is what armies are doing today, here and there, when they pretend to bring freedom to people and do so by dropping 'humanitarian' bombs on them.

Universality doesn't justify the use of force, outside legal confines. But neither does the respect for the individual mean that there are no grounds for common norms. It is not because a practice is deeply rooted in the traditions of a foreign country that it does not deserve to be condemned. Excision is a case in point: a transgression of human rights, it does not warrant armed intervention, but the latter is not the only available means of action. We sometimes forget that, in the not so distant past, our own practices were very different from what they are today. They have changed, not as a result of foreign intervention, but out of internal necessity. Nevertheless, when excision is practised in a country where it is prohibited by law, there is no reason to tolerate it as an expression of cultural specificity. The same is true of the violence inflicted on women (another widespread 'tradition'), ill treatment in prisons and infringement of freedom of expression. To consider that all practices are equally deserving of respect, under pretext of tolerance, is to give up on the idea of the unity of the species and, ultimately, to deem others incapable or unworthy of benefiting from the same treatment that is reserved to us. Equality of rights is not negotiable.

The Age of Enlightenment was characterized by the discovery of the foreignness of others, whether they lived in an earlier time or somewhere else. They were no longer seen as an embodiment of our ideal or as a distant fore-runner of our current perfection, as had been the case at other times. But this recognition of the plurality of the human species is fertile only if it avoids radical relativism and does not prompt us to give up on our common humanity.

eight

The Enlightenment and Europe

THE SPIRIT OF THE ENLIGHTENMENT, AS IT CAN be described today, raises a curious problem. Ingredients of it can be found in various periods in all the world's great civilizations and yet it took hold at a precise point in time – the eighteenth century – and in a particular place – Western Europe. Let us examine these two statements.

To begin with, we cannot help but note that Enlightenment thinking is, in fact, universal, even though it cannot be observed everywhere at all times. This is not only a matter of the practices that presuppose it, but also of a theoretical awareness. Traces can be found of it in

India in the third century BCE in the precepts addressed to emperors and in the edicts issued by the latter. They are found again with the 'freethinkers' of Islam from the eighth to tenth centuries; in Confucianist renewal during the Song dynasty in China from the eleventh to twelfth centuries; and in the movements against slavery in black Africa in the late seventeenth and early eighteenth centuries. Let us enumerate, in no particular order, a few characteristics of this thinking from the most varied places.

Take, for instance, recommendations of religious tolerance, bound up with the plurality of religions practised in a single territory: Brahmanism and Buddhism in India; Confucianism and Buddhism in China; the presence of Muslims, Jews, Christians, Zoroastrians and Manicheans in the Middle East; the co-existence of Islam and pagan traditions in black Africa. Everywhere it was obvious – as will be said often in eighteenth-century Europe – that tolerance was preferable to war and persecutions. Another imperative, probably related to the preceding one, concerns secularism, and the need to separate the political and the theological, the power of the state and that of religion. The desire was to see the society of human beings regulated on the basis of purely human principles – and hence to see power on earth in the hands of the prince rather than in those of intermediaries with the other world.

The plea for autonomy of political power went hand in hand with a desire for autonomy of knowledge. Witness the idea in India that the king must not yield to tradition, to omens or to signs from the stars; that he must trust rational inquiry alone; or yet again the defence by the famous ninth-century Arab doctor, Razi, of strictly human knowledge drawn from experience and framed only by reason. Many technical inventions throughout the history of China testify to an attitude of freedom of research in the field of knowledge; the same is true of scientific progress in the Islamic world in mathematics, astronomy, optics and medicine.

Another equally widespread trait is the very idea of universality, of the equal dignity of all human beings, and of the universal foundations of morality and hence the unity of the human race. 'There is no activity super-ior to furthering good in the world,' declared the Indian emperor Asoka in the third-century BCE. It is this philosophy of universality that was also the starting point of the fight against slavery in Africa. In 1615 Ahmed Baba wrote a treatise arguing for the equality of races and denying the legitimacy of such practices.

These manifestations, which I bring together here somewhat arbitrarily, around what we regard as the spirit of the European Enlightenment, were more or less far-reaching. In India, the recommendation to give priority to rational inquiry over beliefs and superstitions was reserved to the monarch and did not spread to the population at large. If there was any proximity with the Enlightenment, it was in the area of what is known as 'enlightened absolutism'. The Muslim 'freethinkers' were severely repressed from the tenth century on. The most significant comparison can be made with Confucianist teaching in China, which concerns, on principle, a natural and human world: it posits individual improvement as a goal and education and work as the means to it. It is no accident that eighteenth-century European philosophers felt a particular sympathy for the Chinese 'model' (about which they, admittedly, had only a rough idea).

These multiple developments attest to the universality of Enlightenment ideas, over which the Europeans had no monopoly. And yet, it was in Europe in the eighteenth century that this movement gained momentum and that a great synthesis of thought was formulated that later spread across the continents: first in North America, then in Europe itself, in Latin America, in Asia and in Africa. One cannot help wondering why in Europe and not, for instance, in China? Without attempting to find a definitive answer to this difficult question (historical changes are hugely complex phenomena, with multiple, even contradictory causes), it is worth noting one characteristic that existed in Europe and nowhere else – namely, political autonomy, that of the collectivity and of the individual. Such individual autonomy was situated in Europe within the framework of society and not outside of its confines (as was the case for the Indian 'renouncers', mystics in Islamic countries and Chinese monks). What characterizes the European Enlightenment is that it prepared the way for the emergence of both these notions, individual and democracy, together. But why was it precisely in Europe that these ideas could prosper?

The answer to this too can only be complex, yet one thing is plain to see and that is that Europe is at once one and many. Enlightenment thinkers were well aware of this. The European powers formed a kind of system: they were connected by commerce and politics and they were underpinned by the same general principles. This system was based, on the one hand, on the unity of science and the possibility of agreeing on what constitutes progress in the field of knowledge, and, on the other, on a shared ideal, indebted as much to Christian teaching as to the traditions of natural law. Rousseau noted with regret that 'there are no longer any Frenchmen, Germans, Spaniards, or even Englishmen; there are only Europeans'.[80] At the same time, Europeans were equally aware of the differences between their countries and for good reason, since they made the most of these differences. Travelling and living abroad became extremely common if not indispensable. Before embarking on his major work *The Spirit of Laws*, Montesquieu deemed it necessary to travel across Europe and study the customs of different peoples. Charles–Joseph, Prince de Ligne, Austrian field marshal, ambassador to Russia and writer in French, calculated that he had travelled between Brussels and Vienna thirty–four times and had spent more than three years of his life in transit. He concluded, 'I like being a foreigner everywhere, French in Austria, Austrian in France, and Russian everywhere; that is the way to make oneself happy and to be dependent nowhere.'[81]

Foreign countries could be places to learn or to escape persecutions, or they could be sources of stimulation to one's own research. Lavoisier would not have discovered the secret of air and water in France if he hadn't been stimulated by Priestley's parallel discoveries in England. No country stood out in this regard more than the others. Prévost, Voltaire and Rousseau spent time in England; Hume, Bolingbroke and Sterne in France; Winckelmann and Goethe in Italy; Beccaria in France. Voltaire, Maupertuis and La Mettrie left France to find protection from Frederick II in Berlin; and Diderot became Catherine II's adviser in Russia. Plurality is beneficial in and of itself. After having compared the English, the French and the Italians, Voltaire concluded, 'I don't know which one of the three nations is to be preferred; but happy the person who knows their different merits.'[82] He does not, however, reveal to us the reason for this happiness.

What characterizes Europe, compared to other parts of the world, is the large number of states established on its territory. One cannot help being struck by the contrast in comparison with China, for instance, which covers about the same area: a single state on the one hand as against forty-odd independent states on the other. This

multiplicity, which could have been considered a draw-
back, was regarded by Enlightenment thinkers as
Europe's advantage, and they saw the comparison with
China precisely as the most illuminating in this regard. As
Hume put it, 'In China, there seems to be a pretty considerable stock of politeness and science, which, in the
course of so many centuries, might naturally be expected
to ripen into something more perfect and finished, than
what has yet arisen from them. But China is one vast
empire, speaking one language, governed by one law, and
sympathizing in the same manners.'[83] A wellspring that
was inventive and creative at the start was stopped by
the existence of an immense unified empire where
minds were dulled by the uncontested reign of authority,
traditions and established reputations. Contrary to the
old saying, here it is in division that there is strength.
Hume was perhaps the first thinker who saw the identity
of Europe less in a characteristic shared by all (the
heritage of the Roman empire or the Christian religion)
than in its very plurality – not the plurality of individuals
but of the countries that compose it. The question is by
what alchemical process is it possible to convert not so
much mud into gold as a characteristic in itself negative

(difference) into a positive attribute? And how can plurality give rise to unity?

Eighteenth-century thinkers wanted to know what the
advantages of diversity could be and they formulated
several answers, maybe because they were faced with
this question in different fields. To begin with, the most
problematical plurality was that of religions. On the occa-
sion of a trip to The Hague, Voltaire rejoiced at the
tolerance that prevailed there, with no one religion trying
to eliminate the others. Ten years later, during a visit to
England he noted the same advantage of plurality and
concluded, 'Were there but one religion in England, its
despotism would be fearful; were there but two they
would cut each other's throats; but there are thirty and
they live in peace and happiness.'[84] The reasons for this
preference are easy to guess. If one religion occupied a
hegemonic position, its followers would invariably be
tempted to oppress the others, to the point of eliminating
them. The presence of two religions only would cause
rivalry, and the memory of the Wars of Religion and of
the civil wars that caused so much bloodshed in France
was still fresh in everybody's mind. Plurality begins with
the number three and it involves an external agency, a

non-religious authority that ensures peace between them. Hence the need to separate spiritual power and temporal power. Montesquieu was not against religions; he too wanted many of them, because he thought that each tries to instil in its followers good rules of conduct: '[n]ow what is there more capable of animating this zeal than a multiplicity of religions?'[85] Plurality fosters emulation and no amount of goodwill is ever superfluous.

In an essay published in 1742 entitled *Of the Rise and Progress of the Arts and Sciences*, Hume reflects upon what promotes the development of culture, noting that the plurality of states in Europe seems to be a favourable element. The advantage is twofold: these states are not entirely foreign to one another, they are 'connected together by commerce and policy'; at the same time, their plurality creates a space of freedom. Hume discovers that this plurality fosters a critical spirit, whereas unity tends to stifle it. Not only does a vast unified territory require a strong power and create such a distance between the leaders and ordinary citizens that the former tend to be sacralized and considered beyond reproach, but also, in a unified space, an inflated reputation is never the object of criticism, which is why there is a risk that it will be maintained for quite some time. This dire situation is illustrated, as we have just seen, by the case of China, but also by Christianity; the uniform (Catholic) domination of this religion led 'to the utter depravation of every kind of learning'. The Reformation and the recognition of several forms of Christianity marked a turning point in this respect, and the arts and sciences began to flourish as a result.

The plurality of Hume's European space fostered a cautious attitude towards established assertions and reputations. 'Where a number of neighbouring states have a great intercourse of arts and commerce, their mutual jealousy keeps them from receiving too lightly the law from each other, in matters of taste and of reasoning, and makes them examine every work of art with the greatest care and accuracy.' A passing infatuation for a work in Paris may not have much impact in London, Berlin or Milan. If French taste had been imposed by force on all of Europe, nobody would have dared criticize Descartes's science and philosophy. This was not the case, and so his theories were subjected to vigorous criticism outside France, after which they were ousted by Newton's physics, which was subjected in turn to ruthless scrutiny outside

England, and improved in consequence. If, on the other hand, a work manages to make a name for itself abroad, it is a sign of its superior quality, for such a reputation is surely well deserved.

Europe is not the first area to benefit from internal plurality. Ancient Greek culture flourished for this reason. The fact that the Greek city-states were divided by mountain chains guaranteed their independence, while a shared language and interests favoured communication. The result was a balance between plurality and unity. 'Greece was a cluster of little principalities' where 'contention and debates sharpened the wits of men'. The continent where Hume lived was built on the same model. 'Europe is at present a copy at large, of what Greece was formerly a pattern in miniature.' Its superiority arises from what others consider a hurdle. 'Europe, of all the four parts of the world, is the most broken [...] And hence the sciences arose in Greece; and Europe has been hitherto the most constant habitation of them.'[86] Europeans worthy of Hume would be those who are not content with tolerating differences, those who from this absence of identity draw a presence: that of an alert critical spirit that stops at no taboo, that is prepared to examine all traditions impartially, based on what all human beings have in common – namely, reason. In this, he agreed with Montesquieu, whose great political idea was that freedom (and the freedom to criticize is one of its principal forms) requires a plurality of powers rather than a concentration of power in the same hands.

Finally, we have the problem of plurality and its eventual advantages in the political arena of the republic, since the opinions and choices of the citizens composing it are usually quite varied, yet the republic that unites them must speak, in the end, with one voice. The way in which the plurality of individuals is taken into account can be examined to see if it can serve as a model for the co-existence of nations.

Popular sovereignty is embodied in a common will, but what is the relationship between the latter and the will of each individual person? To answer this question, Rousseau introduced a distinction (which has not always been clearly understood) between the general will and the will of all. The will of all is the mechanical sum of individual wills. Its ideal is to be unanimous but its reality is a majority of voices. When opinions diverge, this will is no longer the will of all; to be so, something has to be done to make all agree. In the idea of the will of all lies the seeds of the totalitarian project, wherein all citizens are expected to hold the same ideal, and dissident opinions – when they exist – are repressed and eliminated.

General will, in Rousseau's sense of the term, involves, to the contrary, taking differences into account. The 'generality' of it is to be understood as equality before the law. No citizen is cast aside or held to be inferior to others. 'Any exclusion is a breach of generality.' In what sense is it common to all? It represents, adds Rousseau, the sum of differences of individual wills, the sum of a 'great number of trifling differences'.[87] Here, Rousseau is using the language of infinitesimal calculus as developed by Leibniz. General will is not a sum of identities; it is even opposed to each individual identity and consists in seeking a generality that encompasses differences. Leibniz illustrates this passage from the particular to the general by a comparison between the city as one and the view that its inhabitants have of it: 'a same town seen from different sides appears quite different, as if it presented numerous perspectives'.[88]

Concretely, each citizen has his or her own interests and interests diverge from one individual to another. If we relinquish the idea of forcing people to submit, the only solution is to encourage people to recognize that (like the residents of the city) their perspective is partial, to detach themselves from it (to act 'in the silence of passions', to borrow Diderot's expression[89]), and to position themselves from the standpoint of the general interest. After all, representatives in a democracy are supposed to act in the interest of all even though they have been elected by the voices of only some. This requires seeing things from the point of view of our neighbour, whose opinion differs from our own, trying to reason as the other would in order to be able to adopt a standpoint that takes the difference between others and us into account. Kant, who pursued Rousseau's line of reasoning on this subject, did not think that this was a superhuman task; in fact, it is natural 'to think from the standpoint of everyone else'.[90] Differences would be integrated in this way into a superior form of unity.

The lesson of the Enlightenment consists in saying that plurality can give rise to a new unity in at least three ways: it encourages tolerance through emulation; it develops and protects a critical spirit; and it facilitates self-detachment, which leads to a superior integration of the self and the other. It would be hard not to see how much the European construction today could benefit from this lesson. If it is to succeed, it must not restrict itself to treaties on customs tariffs or to improving bureaucratic structures; it must take on a certain European spirit that the inhabitants of the continent can be proud of. But this raises a problem: what all of the European nations have in common − namely, scientific rationality, defence of the legally constituted state and of human rights − is of universal and not specifically European import. At the same time, this common substratum does not suffice to organize a viable political entity. It has to be completed by particular choices, rooted in each nation's history and culture. The example of language is revealing in this respect: each human group continues to speak in its own language rather than adopting a universal tongue. The existence of an international language of communication − i.e. English nowadays − in no way eliminates the need for particular languages.

Moreover, European nations have witnessed the clash of the most varied ideological options in the course of their long history, and every dominant ideology engendered doctrines that opposed it. Faith is a European tradition but so is atheism, the defence of hierarchy and that of equality, continuity and change, the expansion of the empire and the fight against imperialism, revolution as well as reform and conservatism. European populations are much too diverse to be reduced to a few common elements. In addition, they have received much input from migrant populations who brought their own religions, customs and memories with them. The 'will of all', to borrow Rousseau's expression, cannot be imposed without some Europeans sustaining violent pressure from others, otherwise it would be just a mere pretence, a mask of virtue for purposes of display.

On the other hand, the identity of Europe, and hence its 'general will', could be established, drawing on analyses made during the Age of Enlightenment, and if, instead of isolating one attribute to impute it to all, the status given to our differences were taken as a basis of unity, along with ways of benefiting from them. This could be done by fostering tolerance and emulation, the free exercise of the critical spirit, and the self-detachment that enables individuals to see things from another's standpoint and attain thereby a level of generality that includes both viewpoints. To write an identical history for all Europeans would involve eliminating all sources of discord. The outcome would be a pious history that would hide disagreements and conform to whatever happens to be politically correct at the time. If, on the other hand, one were to attempt to write a 'general' history, then the French would no longer content themselves with studying their history exclusively from their own standpoint; they would take into consideration the way that the Germans, the English, the Spanish, the Algerians or the Vietnamese see the same events. They would discover that their people did not always play the flattering role of hero or victim, and they would be less likely to fall into the Manichean trap of seeing good and evil neatly divided on either side of the border. This is precisely the attitude that Europeans may very well have in common in the future and that they could cherish as their most precious heritage.

The ability to integrate differences without erasing them distinguishes Europe from the world's other great political areas: from India and from China, from Russia and from the United States, where a highly diverse population of individuals makes up a single nation. Europe, for its part, not only recognizes the rights of individuals, but also those of historic, cultural and political communities that are the member states of the union. This understanding was not a gift from heaven; it came with a high price tag: before being the continent that embodies tolerance and mutual recognition, Europe was the site of painful divisions, murderous conflicts and incessant wars. This long experience etched in its memory, in its narratives, in its buildings and even in its landscapes, is the tribute it had to pay to be able to benefit, many years later, from peace.

The Enlightenment is Europe's most prestigious creation and it could never have come to be without the existence of a European space that is at once one and many. But the opposite is also true: Europe, as we conceive it today, has its origins in the Enlightenment. And so it would not be an exaggeration to say that without Europe there would be no Enlightenment and without the Enlightenment there would be no Europe.

A Note of Conclusion

THE ENLIGHTENMENT BELONGS TO THE PAST, since there was an Age of Enlightenment, yet one cannot say that it is 'over' since it has come to designate not only a situated historical doctrine, but also an attitude towards the world. And so it continues to be evoked by authors who, depending on their appreciations, will cite it as the source of all our past and present woes (colonialism, genocide, the rule of selfishness) or call on it for help in fighting present and future vices, in an attempt to 'rekindle the light' or spread it to distant lands and cultures that still have no experience of it. The reason for its topicality is twofold: we are all children of the Enlighten-ment, even when we attack it; at the same time, the ills fought by the spirit of the Enlightenment turned out to be more resistant than eighteenth-century theorists thought. They have even grown more numerous. The traditional adversaries of the Enlightenment — obscu-rantism, arbitrary authority and fanaticism — are like the heads of the Hydra that keep growing back as they are cut. This is because they draw their strength from characteristics of human beings and societies that are as ineradicable as the desire for autonomy and dialogue. People need security and comfort no less than freedom and truth; they would rather defend the members of their group than subscribe to universal values; and the desire for power, which leads to the use of violence, is no less characteristic of the human species than rational argu-mentation. Added to this are modern distortions of the Enlightenment, in the form of scientism, individualism, radical desacralization, loss of meaning and wholesale relativism, to name a few.

There is reason to fear that these attacks will never cease. It is therefore all the more necessary to keep the spirit of the Enlightenment alive. The age of maturity that past authors were hoping would come seems not to be the destiny of humankind: humanity is condemned to seek truth rather than possess it. Asked if we were already living 'in an *enlightened* age', Kant wrote, 'the answer is No, but we do live in an age of *enlightenment*'.[91] This would be the vocation of our species: to pick up the task of enlightenment with each new day, knowing that it is interminable.

Notes

1   TN: The French term for the Enlightenment, *les Lumières*,
    literally means 'the lights'.

2   Turgot, *Tableau philosophique des progrès successifs de l'esprit
    humain* (1750) (Paris: Calmann-Lévy, 1970), 12.

3   Rousseau, *Discourse on the Origin and Foundations of
    Inequality Among Men* (1755), *The Discourses and Other
    Early Political Writings*, ed. Victor Gourevitch (Cambridge
    University Press, 1997), 159, 167, 184, 138.

4   TN: Todorov is referring to the murder of Sohane Benziane,
    17, in October 2002 in the Parisian suburb of Vitry by an 18-
    year-old boy who doused her with petrol and set her on fire
    because she snubbed his advances.

5   Rousseau, 'Lettre sur la vertu, l'individu et la société', Annales
    de la société Jean-Jacques Rousseau 16 (1997), 325.

6   Online source: www.jstor.org/sici?sici=0022-5037
    (198601%2F03)47%3A1%3C61%3AMPOH%3E2.0.CO%3B2-6

7   Montesquieu, The Spirit of Laws, trans. Thomas Nugent (New
    York and London: Hafner Publishing Company, 1966), 3.

8   De Bonald, Législation primitive (Paris: Adrien Le Clère,
    1829), volume 1, 250.

9   Montesquieu, 'Letter to the Marquis de Stanville' (27 May
    1750), Œuvres complètes (Paris: Nagel, 1955), volume 3;
    Rousseau, 'Letter to Beaumont' (1762), Œuvres complètes
    (Paris: Gallimard, 1969), volume 4, 996.

10 Condorcet, Outlines of an historical view of the progress of the
    human mind: being a posthumous work of the late M. de
    Condorcet (Philadelphia: Lang and Uftick, 1796), 253–4.

11 Leroy-Beaulieu, De la colonisation chez les peuples modernes,
    1902, volume 1, xxi, vii.

12 Ferry (1885), Discours et opinions 1893–1898 (Paris: Armand
    Colin & Cie), volume 5, 211.

13 Bugeaud, Par l'épée et par la charrue – écrits et discours (Paris:
    PUF, 1948), 68.

14 Tocqueville (1846), Œuvres complètes (Paris: Gallimard,
    1962), volume 1, 299.

15 Ferry, Discours et opinions 1893–1898, volume 5, 209.

16 Eliot, *The Idea of a Christian Society* (London: Faber and Faber, 1940), 63.

17 Solzhenitsyn, online source: http://www.columbia.edu/cu/augustine/arch/solzhenitsyn/harvard1978.html

18 John Paul II, *Memory and Identity: Conversations at the Dawn of a Millennium* (New York: Rizzoli, 2005), 10, 110.

19 Solzhenitsyn, *op. cit.*

20 John Paul II, *Memory and Identity*, 48, 134–5.

21 Montesquieu, *Treatise on Duties*, online source: http://books.google.com/books?id=x-vDjpV0vrQC&pg=PA179&lpg=PA179&dq=montesquieu+justice+%22human+laws%22+existence+reasonable&source=web&ots=LQ-2MUT8br&sig=78UDHKwikIGD445iSl4qwL8OdHA&hl=en&sa=X&oi=book_result&resnum=3&ct=result; *The Spirit of Laws*, 19.

22 See page 72.

23 Rousseau, *Discours sur l'économie politique* (1756), *Œuvres complètes*, volume 3, 248; Diderot, 'Éclectisme', *Encylopédie*, this translation from online source: http://books.google.com/books?id=5Up1LRv6k3AC&pg=PA122&lpg=PA122&dq=diderot+encyclopedie+eclecticism+philosopher+tradition+%22universal+consent%22&source=web&ots=7e35y1ayO7&sig=aK6S8k7_UVj2rw5ouDy8v3aYBEc&hl=en&sa=X&oi=book_result&resnum=4&ct=result

24 Kant, 'An Answer to the Question: What is Enlightenment?' (1784), *What is the Enlightenment? Eighteenth-Century Answers and Twentieth-Century Questions*, ed. James

Schmidt (Berkeley: University of California Press, 1996), 58; 'What is Orientation in Thought?', *Kant: Political Writings*, ed. H. S. Reiss (Cambridge University Press, 1970), 249.

25 Diderot, 'Fait', *Encylopédie*; Condorcet, *Cinq mémoires sur l'instruction publique* (1791) (Paris: Garnier-Flammarion, 1994), 257; Kant, *The Critique of Pure Reason*, trans. J. M. D. Meiklejohn (Dodo Press, 2007), preface to the first edition.

26 Montesquieu, *The Spirit of Laws*, 154.

27 Rousseau, *An inquiry into the nature of the social contract, or, Principles of political right* (1762), *'The Social Contract' and Other Later Political Writings*, ed. Victor Gourevitch (Cambridge University Press, 1997), III, I and II, 6.

28 Hume, *A Treatise on Human Nature* (1739), online source: http://ebooks.adelaide.edu.au/h/hume/david/h92t/ B2.3.3.html

29 Rousseau, *Dialogues* (1772–6), *The Collected Writings of Rousseau* (Hanover and London: University Press of New England, 1990), volume 1, 118.

30 Rousseau, *The Discourses*, 185.

31 Sade, *Justine, Philosophy in the Bedroom, and Other Writings*, trans. Richard Seaver and Austryn Wainhouse (New York: Grove Weidenfeld, 1965), 283–4.

32 Blanchot, *Lautréamont and Sade*, trans. Stuart and Michelle Kendall (Stanford University Press, 2004), 10, 37.

33 Bataille, *L'Érotisme* (Paris: Minuit, 1979), 192, 210.

34 *Ibid.*

35 Blanchot, *Lautréamont and Sade*, 37.

36 Condorcet, *Cinq mémoires*, 85, 86, 93.

37 Aron, *Memoirs, Fifty Years of Political Reflection*, trans.
George Holoch (New York and London: Holmes and Meier,
1983), 42.

38 Rousseau, *Œuvres complètes*, volume 4, 1072.

39 Beccaria, *An Essay on Crimes and Punishments*, with a
commentary by M. de Voltaire (Edinburgh: Alexander
Donaldson, 1778), 95.

40 Condorcet, *Cinq mémoires*, 93; cf. *Rapport sur l'instruction
publique* (Paris: Edilig, 1989), 254, Engl. transl. *On Public
Instruction*, online source: http://www.familycentered
learning.org/condorcet.txt

41 Condorcet, *Cinq mémoires*, 95.

42 *Ibid.*, 104–5.

43 Gurian, 'Totalitarianism as Political Religion', *Totalitarianism*,
ed. Carl J. Friedrich (New York: Grosset & Dunlap, 1964), 122.

44 *Le Monde*, 10 September 2002.

45 *Ni putes ni soumises* (Paris: La Découverte, 2004), 161.

46 Condorcet, *On Public Instruction*, online source.

47 Hume, *The Sceptic, Essays and Treatises on Several Subjects*
(Edinburgh, 1793), 166.

48 Condorcet, *Rapport sur l'instruction publique*, 251.

49 Condorcet, *Cinq mémoires*, 85–7, 93–4.

50 *Ibid.*, 261.

51 *Ibid.*, 88.

52 Diderot, *Supplement to the Bougainville's 'Voyage'*, *Diderot,
    Interpreter of Nature: Selected Writings*, ed. Jonathan Kemp,
    trans. Jean Stewart and Jonathan Kemp (New York:
    International Publishers, 1936), 181–2.

53 Sade, *Justine, Philosophy*, 323.

54 Condorcet, *Vie de Turgot* (1786), *Œuvres complètes* (Paris:
    Firmin Didot Frères, 1849), volume 5, 203.

55 Rousseau, *Émile*, *Œuvres complètes*, volume 4, 601.

56 Kolakowski, 'Totalitarianism and the Lie', *1984 Revisited*, ed.
    Irving Howe (New York: Harper & Row, 1983).

57 Cited by S. P. Huntington, *Who Are We?* (London: The Free
    Press, 2004), 86–7.

58 Franklin, *Memoirs of the life and writings of Benjamin
    Franklin, L.L.D. F.R.S.* (Philadelphia, [1808–]1818), volume
    1, 100, 113.

59 Diderot, 'Encyclopédie', *Encyclopédie*, volume 5, 642.

60 Rousseau, *Julie, or the New Heloise*, *The Collected Writings of
    Rousseau*, trans. Philip Stewart and Jean Vaché (Hanover and
    London: University Press of New England, 1997), volume 6,
    439.

61 Kant, *Groundwork of the Metaphysics of Morals* (Cambridge and New York: Cambridge University Press, 1998), 37.

62 Pope, *An Essay on Man* (1734) (London: Methuen, 1950), Epistle IV.

63 Voltaire, *Lettres philosophiques* (1734) (Paris: Garnier-Flammarion, 1964), 67.

64 Hume, *Essays and Treatises*, 186.

65 Rousseau, *Émile, Œuvres complètes*, volume 4, 503, 816.

66 Lavoisier, *Pages choisies* (Paris: Éditions Sociales, 1974), 96, 103.

67 Sade, *Justine, Philosophy*, 220.

68 Rousseau, *Émile, Œuvres complètes*, volume 4, 817; 'Lettre sur la vertu, l'individu et la société', 325.

69 *Letters of Joshua Reynolds* (Cambridge University Press, 1929), 18; *Italienische Reise* (1787), *Werke* (Hamburg: Chr. Wegner, 1974), volume 11, 386.

70 Rousseau, *The Discourses*, 188; Rousseau, *An inquiry*, 30.

71 Montesquieu, *The Spirit of Laws*, 237; Rousseau, *An inquiry*, 10; Condorcet (1781), *Œuvres complètes*, volume 7, 69.

72 Montesquieu, *Pensées*, 10, *Œuvres complètes*, 855; Diderot, *Correspondance* (Paris: Éditions de Minuit, 1962), volume 8, 16.

73 Voltaire, *L'A.B.C.* (1768), *Dialogues et anecdotes philosophiques* (Paris: Garnier, 1939), volume 4, 280; Rousseau, *Émile,Œuvres complètes*, volume 4, 547.

74 Wolff, *Principes du droit de la nature et des gens* (1750) (Caen: Bibliothèque de philosophie politique et juridique, 1988), § 68.

75 Beccaria, *An Essay on Crimes and Punishments*, 101, 111.

76 *Ibid.*, 64.

77 Tillion, Letter to Cardinal Feltin, dated 7 December 1957, *Combats de guerre et de paix* (Paris: Éditions du Seuil, 2007), 734.

78 Beccaria, *An Essay on Crimes and Punishments*, 142.

79 Bayle, *De la tolérance. Commentaire philosophique sur ces paroles de Jésus–Christ 'Contrains–les d'entrer'* (Paris: Presses Pocket, 1992).

80 Rousseau, *Considérations sur le gouvernement de Pologne*, *Œuvres complètes*, volume 3, 960.

81 Prince de Ligne, *Lettres écrites de Russie* (1782), 68.

82 Voltaire, *Lettres philosophiques*, 145.

83 Hume, *Essays and Treatises*, 183.

84 Voltaire, *Lettres philosophiques*, 47.

85 Montesquieu, *Persian Letters* (Edinburgh: Alexander Donaldson, 1773), 178.

86 Hume, *Essays and Treatises*, 123.

87 Rousseau, *An inquiry*, 26.

88 Leibniz (1714), *The Monadology*, online source:
http://philosophy.eserver.org/leibniz-monadology.txt

89 Diderot, 'Droit naturel' (1755), *Œuvres complètes*, volume 14.

90 Kant, *The Critique of Judgement*, trans. James Creed Meredith
(Oxford University Press, 1952), 124.

91 Kant, 'An Answer to the Question: What is Enlightenment?'
(1784), *Kant: Political Writings*, 58.